P9-DIA-648

URBAN EVOLUTION

URBAN EVOLUTION

Studies in the Mathematical Ecology of Cities

DIMITRIOS S. DENDRINOS
with HENRY MULLALLY

OXFORD UNIVERSITY PRESS
1985

HT
153
.D44
1985

Oxford University Press, Walton Street, Oxford OX2 6DP

London New York Toronto
Delhi Bombay Calcutta Madras Karachi
Kuala Lumpur Singapore Hong Kong Tokyo
Nairobi Dar es Salaam Cape Town
Melbourne Auckland

and associated companies in
Beirut Berlin Ibadan Mexico City Nicosia

Oxford is a trade mark of Oxford University Press

Published in the United States
by Oxford University Press, New York

© Dimitrios S. Dendrinos and Henry Mullally 1985

All rights reserved. No part of this publication may be reproduced,
stored in a retrieval system, or transmitted, in any form or by any means,
electronic, mechanical, photocopying, recording, or otherwise, without
the prior permission of Oxford University Press

This book is sold subject to the condition that it shall not, by way
of trade or otherwise, be lent, re-sold, hired out or otherwise circulated
without the publisher's prior consent in any form of binding or cover
other than that in which it is published and without a similar condition
including this condition being imposed on the subsequent purchaser

British Library Cataloguing in Publication Data

Dendrinos, Dimitrios, S.
Urban evolution: studies in the mathematical
ecology of cities.
1. Cities and towns – Mathematical models
I. Title   II. Mullally, Henry
307.7'6'0724   HT153

ISBN 0-19-823249-7

Library of Congress Cataloging in Publication Data

Dendrinos, Dimitrios S.
Urban evolution.
Bibliography: p.
Includes index.
1. Urbanization – Mathematical models. 2. Cities
and towns – Growth – Mathematical models.
3. Ecology – Mathematical models. 4. Population
– Mathematical models.   I. Mullally, Henry.
II. Title.
HT153.D44 1984   307.7'6'0724   84-25571

ISBN 0-19-823249-7

Set by Grestun Graphics, Oxford
and printed in Great Britain by
Biddles Ltd., Guildford

JUL 1 1985

To Iris and Spiros Dendrinos

PREFACE

The main point of this book is that, while the underlying processes in urban dynamics may be very complicated, the macroscopic state of the urban system is simple, easily described and understood. Urban settings are shown to have internal clocks manifested by regular cycles developed within particular environments. A set of non-linear dynamic models based on the Volterra–Lotka[†] formalism, appropriately adapted, are shown to account for certain basic qualitative features of urban systems. This formalism is particularly useful for analysing aspects of dynamic stability. Although the methodology of mathematical ecology is selectively used in this book, no substantive equivalences with general ecology are made. Using empirical evidence, the book develops the thesis of a dynamic interconnectance among the components of the urban dynamic structure, so that non-linearities, multiplicity of equilibria, and bifurcations in urban dynamics are highlighted.

A major theme in the book is that model complexity often implies dynamical instability, a result known in mathematical ecology through the work of Robert May. This complexity vs. stability issue is central in modelling and understanding urban evolution. Recorded inter-urban growth patterns, extensively discussed in this book, exhibit stability which is attributed to highly selective interconnectance among interacting cities. Whereas, the cause for observed intra-urban instability must be found in an extensive random interdependence among various land uses and zones within cities. Both, inter-urban stability and intra-urban instability are demonstrated in a relative growth framework. A number of insights can be drawn from such an approach, and they are extensively analysed in the book.

Certain epistemological topics in urban evolution are also outlined, as they emerge by approaching urban dynamics from the perspective of mathematical ecology. Urban determinism and stochasticity, selection and optimization, fast and slow urban adaptation are concepts defined and reviewed in a Darwinian framework.

Although direct analogues with general ecology are avoided, the common method forces certain fundamental equivalences in the way

---

[†] In the ecological literature the models are referred to as 'Lotka–Volterra'. In the field of mathematics, Hirsch and Smale (1974), for example, they are referred to as 'Volterra–Lotka'. The latter is adopted here.

problems are stated. As a result of intense theoretical efforts during the past sixty or so years, reinforced by an even longer empirical tradition, general ecology has accumulated a considerable body of principles and methods. Consequently, the preponderant flow of ideas at this stage is from general ecology to urban ecology. As the latter grows, however, the traffic may become more balanced, with questions and solutions in the urban sphere stimulating research in general ecology, much as the work of Darwin was influenced by the writing of Malthus. Ecologists' theoretical efforts can gain significantly from an examination of the economic literature, and in particular that of Samuelson (1948), Hotelling (1929), etc., and the geographic literature, Christaller (1933) and Lösch (1937) among others.

Great care must be exercised in applying concepts or methods developed in one field to problems in a different area. One must ask whether a question pertinent to ecological theory is relevant to urban ecology; and whether other questions not useful to general ecology are pertinent for urban ecology. However, the second task seems more formidable than the first. Almost all theoretical insights that can be obtained using the basic tool of mathematical ecology, namely the Volterra–Lotka formalism, have in all likelihood, already been discovered, in spite of few surprises, e.g. Gilpin (1979). Instead of re-inventing the wheel, the next fruitful source for innovative urban work must come from empirical studies, the source of possibly new phenomena to be identified.

From an urban perspective it is quite surprising that the great advances in the theory of mathematical ecology have gone mostly unnoticed. Here this void is partly filled. It is not accomplished by a wholesale transfer of concepts from ecology to urban dynamics, but rather by a judicious selection of certain basic methodological notions which, when coupled with empirical evidence, provide the main features of an urban theory. One is indeed astonished at the parallel development of the two fields with so many methodological commonalities, and yet so little interaction. Whether this is an example where stability in the evolution of a field requires isolation from other areas of investigation, as increasing connectivity with other disciplines possibly creates instability, remains to be seen.

One, by reading this book, might detect a bias toward description of recorded phenomena, rather than explanation. If so, a comment is in order. Social science events, due to their underlying complexity, whatever that may imply, have multiple suggested explanations. Interest or opinions among researchers on these possible explanations is in general unevenly distributed, but not highly skewed towards one of them. Thus, the value of explanation may not be as high as that of describing an event, particularly if that description is novel.

The book is addressed to social scientists in general, and those in particular with a background in geography, urban and regional science, and urban demography. It could also be of interest to ecologists. Economists, mathematicians, and systems analysts interested in applications of non-linear dynamics may also find certain elements of the book relevant to their disciplines. The book can be used by advanced level undergraduates or entry level graduate students with some background in differential equations. Although some mathematical analysis is included in proving most of the statements made, the mathematical exposition of the main text has been kept to a minimum with most of the key proofs supplied as appendices. The book's main purpose is to serve as a research source, since in many instances it only posits problems without going very deeply into them, leaving the interested reader to develop them further.

D.S.D., H.M.

ACKNOWLEDGEMENTS

Interaction with a number of colleagues from many universities in the US and Europe was essential in shaping the basic concepts found here. Further, their support in publishing this book was instrumental. Since they are so many, alas, all cannot be mentioned.

Drs Robert Holt, from the Department of Systematics and Ecology of the University of Kansas, and Michael Sonis, from the Department of Geography of Bar-Ilan University, have read the entire manuscript. They provided very helpful and insightful comments which aided in improving the book. Their suggestions are deeply appreciated. One of the authors (DSD) wishes, also, to recognize the collaborative work undertaken with Dr Gunter Haag, from the Department of Theoretical Physics of the University of Stuttgart, reported partially in the intra-urban dynamics part of the book.

Helpful comments were also supplied from the reviewers of Oxford University Press. Mr Andrew Schuller, our editor and the editorial staff from OUP, put a signficant amount of time and effort toward the publication of this volume, and for their care and support we deeply thank them together with the Delegates of OUP. Some of the work appearing in this book was supported by the US Department of Transportation and the National Science Foundation.

None of the above, however, is responsible for any remaining errors, shortcomings, or the views held in the book for which we retain full responsibility.

For their time spent in typing and retyping the entire manuscript and their goodwill in doing so, we thank Vonda Kaye Smith and Theresa Bangs.

Permission for reproducing Fig. II.5 has been obtained from the Martinus Nijhoff Publishing Company.

CONTENTS

LIST OF FIGURES

LIST OF TABLES

INTRODUCTION

As an introduction to the book, some broad statements on how one can approach the construction of a theory of urban evolution are made first, and the reasons for the particular path followed are then laid out. An outline of strategic and tactical models sets the stage for the work to be presented. Then, the structure of the book is provided. Finally, certain key terms and their definitions are supplied.

Towards constructing a theory of urban evolution

A theory of urban evolution and its method can be formulated from a number of very distinct perspectives. One might start from a very microscopic level, that of the behaviour of a single individual, and climb up through a series of aggregations to a very macroscopic level. By stating a dynamic theory of micro-behaviour one then might be able to arrive at a dynamic theory of macro- (urban, regional) evolution. Even were such a monumental task feasible, it would not be an efficient undertaking. This book is premised on the belief that in spite of their micro-level complexity basic insights into urban evolution could be obtained by making relatively few, strategically placed, macro-level observations of urban growth and form. It suffices that these observations be made at particular time-periods, and be generic ones, in the sense that they contain if not all at least most of the important qualitative features of urban evolution. Thus, an alternative to the microscopic approach is adopted here. A partial and local view is taken on the subject from a macro-level although reference to micro-level behaviour is made. Specifically, the aggregate dynamic behaviour of cities from the United States is examined as it is manifested in the collective dynamic behaviour of their population.

Over centuries of metropolitan evolution a recurring feature is that of urban cycles. Although a host of factors obviously affect the dynamics of any particular city at any particular time-period (may be too numerous to fully account in a model), urban population and income seem to be most important. Looked at in isolation, population and income oscillate. Considered in combination, urban population and income behave according to a simple and regular dynamic: a damped cyclical motion. Data covering approximately one hundred years indicate that urban oscillations occur at the inter-urban level, obeying certain regularities. Within this time-scale, the cities of the US are characterized by properties of.dynamic stability. More drastic events occur if one considers obviously much longer time-horizons: cities suddenly appear, grow, and then possibly become extinct. Some cities' growth is consistently associated with others' decline. Naturally, these aggregate urban dynamic patterns of various time-scales must not be haphazard or random. Some simple mathematical models of Volterra–Lotka type seem to adequately describe such events.

At the intra-urban level, some isolated but key phenomena from US intra-metropolitan recent history (the past forty-year period) seem to indicate dynamic instability. Empirical evidence regarding the qualitative aspects of the widely discussed phenomena of suburbanization, slum formation, gentrification, etc., seems to point to models capable of producing bifurcating behaviour and switches from stable to unstable equilibria. Bifurcations occur when certain qualitative properties of dynamic equilibria change suddenly over time, when smooth changes in key parameters take place, and certain thresholds are crossed. A host of inter- and intra-urban events can be captured through such bifurcations.

The mathematical ecology-based models presented here address dynamic non-linear interdependencies, stability and multiple equilibria, conditions argued to be necessary components of urban systems theory and modelling. These advances are carried out in a manner which *allows for an analytical treatment*. In these models phenomena of particular interest, including bifurcation in behaviour, can be captured analytically and be verified empirically. This is where the novelty of this work lies.

As will be seen later, some isolated earlier attempts do exist in the geographic literature where non-linear dynamic models have been proposed. Very few are empirically verified. An extensive literature also exists in the urban planning and regional science fields on large-scale urban models. With very few exceptions, these models are static and equilibrium bound and they do not possess analytical solutions. They are also not problem oriented, i.e. they do not address particular urban phenomena or events. A few dynamic models also exist in the urban economic literature, as will be indicated later in the text. They, however, are not empirically tested, and not capable of capturing bifurcating behaviour. Obviously this book is not a forum for a comprehensive review of this particular issue. A comparative study of models found in the various disciplines mentioned with the ecological construct will have to wait. The task here is to lay the foundations for the development of an urban mathematical ecology theory and leave comparisons and/or integration to future studies.

In summary, the main objectives of the book are to show that in spite of their underlying complexity metropolitan dynamics at a macro-scale seem to be consistent with certain simple but powerful population models of the Volterra–Lotka type. These models can be used to obtain basic insights into the topic of urban evolution, to classify a rather broad selection of urban phenomena, and to demonstrate that bifurcation theory provides a means to extend the urban ecological field. By combining these fields of study one can bring the topic of urban evolution closer to the mainstream of the general theory of evolution and possibly contribute to the present epistemological debate regarding smooth and abrupt evolutionary change, determinism and stochasticity, necessity and chance in urban and other social or biological or natural events.

A note on models

Over the past thirty years or so, the relevance of mathematical modelling has been debated in a variety of fields. Empirical and theoretical ecologists, applied and theoretical economists, urban policy-makers and urban theorists, to mention but a few, have extensively debated the issue. Still, the relevance of model-building remains a source for confusion and disagreement. Criticism is fuelled when the dichotomy between micro- (disaggregate) and macro- (aggregated) models is made, mostly centring on the relevance of macro-models. It is even further heated when the use of small versus large dimensionality models is discussed.

Clearly, the two dimensions of the discussion are different. One can have a low dimensionality disaggregated model, or a large dimensionality aggregated one. The use of macro-models, according to this book, lies in the way that one interprets such models. In Part IV of this volume, the epistemological insights gained by such models are provided. This is only one part of the answer. The other, of course, is that knowledge is gained by studying the regular patterns of aggregate behaviour, so that micro-level expectations can be based on macro-system performance. This is further elaborated in Part III.

More critical in the discussion is the low versus high dimensionality argument. It relates to whether a complex system needs a complex (high dimensionality) model to simulate it. In general, low dimensionality models are *strategic* means toward understanding the functioning of social systems. Low dimensionality models are *tactical* means for intervention. This dichotomy has been well recognized in the field of mathematical ecology (May, 1973). Field-workers routinely associate implementation models with complexity, meaning that models of intervention must include a large number of variables and must be disaggregated in order to replicate 'reality' to a meaningful degree. Reality is construed by such analysts as an assortment of a large number of variables.

One can dispute, however, such a definition of reality and instead view reality as the vast collection of locally interconnected subsystems. A meaningful replication of such a reality would require a careful replication of the behaviour of these subsystems in an efficient manner depending on what problem the analyst wished to investigate. Thus, the legitimacy of the call for large-scale systems analysis as a prerequisite for replicating reality can be questioned. In particular this is so when the system exhibits stable behaviour, and multidimensionality induces modelling instability. This is the key problem in building large-scale urban models, meaning models with a large number of interacting variables. Smale (1966) and May (1973) have shown that under particular conditions regarding connectivity such constructs have a built-in property of exhibiting elements of instability into the simulated system. Since certain urban systems have been shown to be relatively stable over extended time-horizons, this type of model-building is clearly inappropriate for such systems. For this book this is a main theme. It is this simple but very powerful proposition which should compel the analyst to construct simple models of low dimensionality and connectivity, at certain instances, even if tactical models are called for. Variety of performance is, further, not limited by small dimensionality. It is of interest here to refer to May's work (1974) which shows that even simple dynamic models are capable of producing a rich variety of behaviour, which at times is indistinguishable from random.

Many analysts have suggested that we take strategic urban models and 'complexify' them by either increasing the number of variables these models have (connecting many subsystem models with one another), or by exhaustively disaggregating the variables in these models. Any attempt to transform strategic models into tactical ones by such artificial means is bound to result at best in misleading and in all likelihood unreliable conclusions. It will become clear to readers of this work that such 'practicalization' of theoretical models is unwise. Implementation models could be constructed, employing *different* variables from the strategic ones but not necessarily *more* variables. In many instances, for a meaningful policy-making function, what is needed is a large number of tactical models with a small number of variables and not one (or a small number of) tactical model(s) with a large number of variables. The advanced mathematics and desired analytical properties which are found in strategic models can also be used in tactical ones.

The structure of the book

The book is divided into four parts. Part I reviews certain basic non-linear, dynamic urban phenomena and some major themes of dynamic stability. The theory of bifurcation and its insights are discussed as the sources for establishing the major qualitative insights of phase transition in the behaviour of a dynamical system. Three specific systems of differential equations (the Volterra–Lotka, Van der Pol equation, and the Hopf bifurcation, and the May–Li–Yorke chaos) are reviewed. They provide the blocks upon which the mathematical exposition of the urban ecological framework is built.

Part II presents the new urban ecological theory and introduces the topic of inter-urban evolution. It analyses and interprets the Volterra–Lotka formalism and elaborates upon the topics of relative urban growth, and urban landscapes of different geographies and economies. Issues of stability and bifurcation are addressed. Bifurcations are viewed, partly, as transitions from one part of the landscape to another. Single as well as multiple urban populations interactions are discussed and the major theme of complexity–instability in inter-urban connectivity is developed. Empirical evidence is supplied to demonstrate the validity of the urban ecological model-drawing from observed phenomena in the dynamic behaviour of the urban sector of the United States. The main elements of formulating the dynamics of an urban hierarchy are discussed. Finally, the issue of optimality in urban ecology is addressed.

Part III views selective topics of intra-urban dynamics. Contrary to the inter-urban case, intra-urban evolution is characterized by instability. Methodological and substantive implications of this presupposition are drawn. The phenomena of suburbanization, neighbourhood tipping, and gentrification among others as observed in the US, are viewed within a framework of bifurcating behaviour in intra-metropolitan dynamics. A theoretical construct is supplied for cyclical land use density–land rent interactions. Deterministic as well as stochastic equation formulations are presented. Conclusions are drawn regarding the use of probabilistic models in urban dynamics. In both Parts II and III policy matters are discussed as they pertain to the dynamics and structural stability elements of urban structure.

Part IV sketches an epistemology of urban dynamics and evolution. Drawing from the richness of the Darwinian paradigm, aspects of selection are elaborated as favouring stability in inter-urban dynamics and instability in intra-urban ecology. May's complexity v. stability argument is utilized in structuring the discussion. Fast and slow motions in urban systems behaviour are viewed as environment adjustment and adaptation processes. Governing these dynamics are least-effort-type optimization integrals capturing different time-scale effects. The search algorithm embedded in the optimization process is viewed as the source for randomness in urban evolution. Coding, replication, and selection issues associated with the algorithm are addressed together with the topic of innovation. Stochasticity and determinism are juxtaposed as modes of theorizing about urban systems. The view is advanced that determinism is the efficient manner by which to study urban dynamics at the scale of urban systems presented here. Aspects of prediction in urban modelling are addressed. Finally, in the Epilogue a few thoughts are given on the connectance between urban analysis and natural sciences.

Some definitions

In the exposition to follow three terms will be extensively used and, although their notions might be closely related, they denote different concepts. 'Oscillatory or periodic motion' will be used to identify a certain movement which is associated with a deterministic regular process. 'Fluctuations' will be a term used to denote the presence of irregularly repeated stochastic or random motion. 'Perturbation' will be employed to indicate rare random shock or disturbance in either a steady state or an equilibrium path. All three are associated with various aspects of non-linear motion.

An urban system (either at the intra- or inter-urban level) is connected with other urban systems. A particular set of interconnected urban systems constitutes a 'community of interacting urban systems'. Depending on the level of spatial disaggregation used, the composition of this community may change. Each community of interacting urban systems contains a particular form of interaction among its members, found in the 'community interaction matrix'. Simply 'community matrix' will denote the coefficients of interaction; whereas the 'community interaction matrix' will denote the Jacobian of the system.

Here in a relative (closed system) framework, 'environment' is used to denote a community of interacting systems at a particular spatial disaggregation. All factors influencing the composition of the community as well as the community interaction matrix constitute the environment of the community within which a particular urban system's behaviour is observed. Thus, the information contained in a particular environment is coded in the specific community composition and interconnectance found in the community interaction matrix.

'Equilibrium' will be used to denote either a singular point or a path (trajectory) towards the singular point, which in certain instances will be referred to as 'steady state' or 'dynamic equilibrium'.

Throughout the text the terms 'development' and 'evolution' are used to denote distinctly different events. Development is used to depict a time-process of successful states of the system along a particular trajectory associated with a dynamic equilibrium. For example, a spiralling sink trajectory identifies a developmental path. Evolution is used to denote transition phases in the nature of the dynamic equilibrium. For example, when a spiralling sink dynamic equilibrium is transformed into a spiralling source by a parameter change, then this phenomenon of transition is referred to as an evolutionary change. This is another point where urban dynamics may differ from the biologist's use of the term 'evolution'.

The terms 'city', 'town', 'urban setting', 'urban area', or 'metropolitan area' are used in the text interchangeably. There are various census definitions for certain of the above which can be overlooked for the purposes of this book. The empirical work refers to the US Census Bureau notion of a Standard Metropolitan Statistical Area (SMSA) and this is what is implied by all these terms. Use of the notions 'region' and 'nation' is made so that a nation can be viewed as a region, but not vice versa. Income and factor reward are used interchangeably. Actually, income is only a part of the more comprehensive notion of 'factor reward', which could include non-income captured variables. Per capita income is used only as a proxy to factor reward, as it is readily available.

In the empirical findings regarding the inter-urban section of the text, it must be noted that, statistical analysis has not been carried out in any formal sense. There are four reasons for this. First, the existing statistical techniques available apply mostly to linear models. Good tests of significance for non-linear models of the type discussed here are still under development. Second, the field of non-linear parameter estimation under the presence of bifurcating points is a fast-growing field and any attempt to use at this stage such methods would run the risk of unduly shifting the focus of this study. The reader is directed to Bennett (1980), Mehra (1980), and Cobb (1981) for some key work on these issues. Third, most of the models discussed here are strategic, so that replicating precisely numerical evidence is not as important as replicating the qualitative features of the evidence presented. Fourth, in many instances data are still not available in extended time-series. In the inter-urban case as more data become available statistical tests must be performed to validate the statements made out of preliminary indications gained by computer simulation as compared with actual values. In the case of intra-urban dynamics, the qualitative phenomena addressed need much more extensive data collection and hypothesis testing.

Part I.

NON-LINEAR DYNAMICAL ANALYSIS
AND STABILITY

A. INTRODUCTION

Part I surveys a range of methods and concepts in non-linear dynamics the use of which will subsequently be evoked to analyse a variety of urban processes. Selection of these topics is intended to convey basic principles and features shared by particular events to be presented, and also provide a set of dynamic models which possesses the ability to supply fundamental qualitative insights into the nature of dynamical systems in general and urban systems in particular.

At the outset, a few notes are made regarding dynamic and structural stability, local and global analysis, deterministic and stochastic behaviour. An introduction to systems of differential equations and logistic growth follows and in particular the Volterra–Lotka system is discussed. Then the phenomenon of bifurcation in behaviour is presented with a reference to the Hopf bifurcation in the Van der Pol equation. Bifurcation in simple difference equations models producing chaotic behaviour is discussed next, based on the May model. Some reference is made on how to use this model in economic analysis. Finally, the topic of structural stability within the framework of catastrophe theory is presented.

For our purpose, in constructing a dynamic model of an inter- or intra-urban system we must assess several things: first, the essential components to be included in the model; second, the mathematical character of the interactions among these components; third, the degree to which the system is closed or open, i.e. its interaction with and composition of the environment; fourth, the mechanism and type of possible perturbations that may shock the system; and finally, and most important, the sought-after qualitative feature(s) we want to replicate. The model to be built must be parsimonious, i.e. the minimum information required to produce efficiently the desired outcome is exclusively utilized.

One must ask the above questions and follow the efficiency rules of model construction when confronted with issues such as: how is the growth and decline of cities, in both absolute and relative terms, related to national growth; what makes a city dominate a nation's economy; are interdependencies in the form of externalities the key to limiting urban growth/decline; is neighbourhood conversion associated only with inter- or intra-group attraction/repulsion; and under what conditions is urban revitalization possible. In developing a model of any topic such as these, one must incorporate into the dynamical analysis appropriate non-linear interdependencies which would produce multiplicity of state. Linear models cannot, in general, incorporate interdependencies with multiple equilibria.

The field of non-linear systems analysis is currently in a phase of explosive growth, and much of it involves areas of pure mathematics inaccessible to many. In this Part, we explore a sample of elementary but interesting and fundamental dynamical behaviours produced by non-linearities. In addition, we lay the groundwork for a kind of analytical approach that will be used throughout the text. There is a sequence of questions one must ask of dynamical models: does an equi- librium exist with each component in a steady state; what does this steady state look like and how does it relate to the environment; does the system return to its equilibrium after a small perturbation; what happens under a large perturbation; and does the system show oscil- latory behaviour. Before looking at particular urban systems, we will attempt to provide a forum for addressing these questions within the framework of dynamical analysis.

Fundamental in the discussion to follow is the distinction between dynamic and structural stability. Dynamic stability addresses the phenomena associated with slight changes in the system's state variables, normally close to an equilibrium. Structural stability is associated with infinitesimal changes in the system's parameters (control variables) as to the effects they have on the behaviour of the system (state variables). In economics, the latter is referred to as comparative statics analysis. The dimensionality of the model affects critically the researcher's ability to carry out analytically structural stability analysis, if one is interested in the global properties of the system.

Very often the analysis presented is restricted to the planar case. This reflects both the practical advantages of being able to illustrate many of the ideas diagrammatically, and also the fact that for dimensions greater than two many of these dynamic models lose their dynamic stability properties when considered over very wide ranges of values. The structural stability of the system (the changes in dynamic stability properties under critical changes in the system's relevant parameters) becomes not only analytically elusive, but, even more important, the chance of obtaining structurally stable systems in n-dimensions is in general very small.

It is not to be concluded that the dimensionality of these models is necessarily a liability in modelling systems seemingly complex (meaning of high dimensionality and interconnectance). Rather, it is an indication of how appropriate such a model is when there is evidence regarding the stability properties of the original system under investigation. For purposes of convenience, in this book stability will mean 'dynamic stability' unless otherwise noted.

Once the dynamic model is constructed, by a system of simultaneous differential (or difference) equations claiming to mimic some aspects of the real world, the most interesting qualitative property concerns the existence and stability of the equilibrium. A number of different definitions of stability exist. Usually, stability analysis refers to the behaviour of a system in the vicinity of an equilibrium point, i.e. neighbourhood stability. In general, a state is said to be stable if, following a small perturbation, it returns to equilibrium. If it departs still further, it is said to be unstable, and if it remains in a displaced state which is determined by the magnitude of the perturbation it is considered to be neutrally stable.

If the model which characterizes the system at hand is linear, the process of evaluating the stability properties of the equilibrium points is fairly straightforward, for global and local properties of the system coincide. However, if the underlying model is non-linear, as is likely to be the case in the urban field, then the situation is more complicated. The equilibrium in a non-linear system need not be a point, as it is with a linear system; it might be a trajectory leading to a steady pattern of oscillations. Usually that is what is meant by a 'dynamic equilibrium'.

In the case where stability analysis refers to a stochastic rather than a deterministic environment then the stability could be manifested in a periodic motion. This motion might be uniquely associated with a range of randomly generated disturbances built into the model and equilibrium solutions are tied into the values which fluctuate about a specific means with specified variances. Such models are not purely stochastic; they must be referred to as quasi-stochastic. The models presented here are mostly deterministic and this reflects a basic bias underlying this volume. At the scale of (inter- or intra-urban) systems examined, deterministic models are found to be good enough approximations and useful to construct in order to replicate the main elements of urban behaviour.

Finally, there are certain models which, although deterministic in their structure, are capable of generating seemingly stochastic and at times chaotic behaviour. Under particular values of their parameters, it can be shown that these models generate what can be construed as random outcomes. Here the term random implies non-repetitive (by the model) patterns, although the pattern *in toto* is precisely replicated by subsequent runs of the model through computer simulation. Thus one must consider these models deterministic, from a broader perspective. Next, few of the main dynamical models and their stability aspects are discussed.

B. SELECTED SYSTEMS OF DIFFERENTIAL EQUATIONS

Any set of ordinary differential equations is referred to as a dynamical system. Many of the most relevant results of n-dimensional dynamical systems can be obtained in the two-dimensional case. In general, one can state the n-dimensional system as

$$\frac{d}{dt} x = F(x); x = (x_1, x_2, \ldots x_n)', F = [F_1(x), F_2(x) \ldots F_n(x)].$$

It is always assumed that the functions $F(x)$ have the necessary weak analytic properties which result in the following

(a)   The system above possesses a unique solution $x^* = x(t)$ satisfying the initial condition $x(0) = x^o$. This solution is referred to as an equilibrium path of the system. Asterisk denotes a quantity evaluated at equilibrium.

(b)   Through each part of R^n there passes a unique trajectory of the system. Two trajectories never cross.

For even the simplest of all dynamic systems it is often difficult to obtain an explicit solution. Instead, effort is put into developing a qualitative theory in which the topological nature of the model's equilibrium point is studied. The focus below is on local stability, since that is what one is likely to be involved with in urban dynamic modelling. The equilibrium values are obtained when motion ceases

$$F[x^*(t)] = 0.$$

Letting $x_i(t) = x_i^* + \epsilon_i(t)$ and expanding the Taylor series around the equilibrium x_i^*, discarding second- and higher-order terms yields the linearized approximation

$$\frac{d}{dt} x = Ax(t)$$

where the stability setting Jacobian matrix A has elements a_{ij}

$$a_{ij} = \left(\frac{\partial F_i}{\partial x_j}\right) \Big|_{x^*}; \quad i, j = 1, 2, \ldots, n.$$

The solution to the above system is

$$x(t) = C \exp(\lambda t)$$

where the matrix C contains constants which depend on the initial values; and λ is the vector of the eigenvalues of A. The latter determine the dynamic behaviour of the system near equilibrium. The linearized vector field near enough to the equilibrium point (the matrix A), describes the connectance of the system's variables as well as the stability properties of the equilibria. The eigenvalues are obtained by solving

$$(A - \lambda I)x = 0$$

where I is the $n \times n$ identity matrix. The system possesses a non-trivial solution if and only if the characteristic polynomial is zero, that is

$$\det(A - \lambda I) = 0$$

a nth order polynomial in the eigenvalues λ, which are complex numbers of the form $\lambda = \alpha + \beta i$. The real part α induces either growth or decay (depending on its sign: positive is growth, whereas negative implies decay). The imaginary part is responsible for oscillatory motion. If all eigenvalues have negative real parts then the perturbations from equilibrium die away in time; if any eigenvalue has a positive real part then the system is locally unstable, or the unstable variable associated with that particular eigenvalue will have exponential growth and will drive the system away from equilibrium over time. If one (or more) eigenvalues have zero real parts (pure imaginary) and all others have negative real parts the system is neutrally stable. A key property of the characteristic polynomial is that the sum of the real part of all eigenvalues equals the sum of the diagonal elements of the matrix A. This is a property of particular interest to conservative systems, as will become clear later in the text.

1. *The Volterra–Lotka system*

Consider the two-dimensional system

$$\frac{dx}{dt} = f(x, y)$$

$$\frac{dy}{dt} = g(x, y).$$

The r.h.s. of this system does not include time explicitly. Therefore, by plotting the results one obtains the phase portrait in the (x, y) plane. The curves $f(x, y) = g(x, y) = 0$ are referred to as isoclines. Any trajectory will cross an f and a g isocline vertically and horizontally correspondingly, except at points where the isoclines intersect – the equilibria of the system. In Appendix I, an example of a simple linear system is shown and the phase portraits corresponding to the various eigenvalues are presented.

One of the most widely discussed examples of a non-linear system in two dimensions is the Volterra–Lotka model of predator–prey ecological interaction which will be presented below for exposition purposes. The model may be represented as

$$\frac{dx}{dt} = x(a - by)$$

$$\frac{dy}{dt} = y(cx - d)$$

where x and y represent the prey and predator populations respectively and $a, b, c, d > 0$. The first equation implies that the growth-rate of the prey is negatively related to the size of the predator population, while the second equation implies that the growth of the predators is positively related to the population of prey. If $y = 0$ the prey population grows exponentially, while if $x = 0$ the predators disappear. The only positive equilibrium is at $(x^* = d/c)$, $(y^* = a/b)$.

Inspecting the linearized vector field of this point

$$A = \begin{bmatrix} a - by^* & -bx^* \\ cy^* & cx^* - d \end{bmatrix} = \begin{bmatrix} 0 & -bd/c \\ ca/b & 0 \end{bmatrix}$$

From this, one obtains the roots $\lambda_i = \pm i\sqrt{(ad)}$. The linearized system is a centre: the system oscillates indefinitely with amplitudes around the equilibrium point depending upon the starting values for x and y, i.e. the equilibrium is neutrally stable. Introduction of limiting factors to growth due to friction in population size (in either or both x, y) results in a radical change in the qualitiative behaviour of the system: the damping element drives the system to an equilibrium where either or both x, y are positive. The system is thus not structurally stable. None the less, Berlinski (1976) characterizes the Volterra–Lotka model as an entity which epitomizes the best use of the differential approach in modelling: even though closed-form solutions cannot be obtained, our comprehension of what it implies for the behaviour of the variables x and y is extensive. The volume of information gained from such a very small-scale model of reality makes it extremely efficient.

Ecologists do not accept that communities can exhibit neutral stability; they are, however, confronted with cases in which periodic stability is at times present. In mathematical ecology such periodic movements can be attributed to non-linearities producing stable limit cycles (as shown in Part II, D.2); or in the case of three or more species interaction, Gilpin (1979); or through stochastic noise in damped oscillations, Nisbet and Gurney (1982), producing 'quasi-cycles.'

Although the predator–prey Volterra–Lotka system is one of the most widely used in mathematical ecology (together with the model depicting competition among species), Volterra analysed a plethora of other interaction models in the early development of mathematical ecology. For a view of these seminal dynamic models the reader is directed to Scudo and Ziegler (1978). In these early essays Volterra set the stage for a comprehensive examination of conservative and dissipative dynamic interaction models. An extensive development of conservative systems is found in Goel *et al.* (1971). The structure of these models follows a definition of functions F_i in

$$\dot{x}_i = x_i F_i.$$

Most frequently, F_i is a linear function of x_i's. Conservative systems by Volterra satisfy the condition

$$\sum_i \sum_j a_{ij} x_i x_j = 0; \quad i,j, = 1, 2, \ldots, n,$$

where a_{ij} are fixed coefficients. This is a conservation expression interpreted by Volterra as 'interaction' among different populations *in toto* and equal to zero. Direct consequences from such a conservation condition are that the community matrix (a_{ij}) is anti-symmetric $(a_{ij} + a_{ji} = 0)$ and that its diagonal elements are zero $(a_{ii} = 0)$. The later implies that there are no squared (friction) terms. The conservation condition adopted by Volterra forced him into accepting that existence of a non-zero equilibrium hinges upon whether there are an even or odd number of interacting species. In the case of an even number of interacting species an equilibrium may exist; it does not exist when an odd number of species interacts. As the elements of the diagonal matrix are all zero, the equilibrium, at best, is neutrally stable (orbits). This occurs when all eigenvalues have zero real parts. If one eigenvalue has a non-zero real part then the system is unstable. This has been a source for discomfort among mathematical ecologists through the years. In Part II, F.1 some new ideas regarding urban conservation conditions which bypass such difficulties (due to their formulation) will be shown.

In ecology, dissipative dynamic interacting species models are the rule. They contain friction terms $(a_{ii} \neq 0)$, and thus they are not conservative. Volterra showed an interest in conservative systems because he was able to identify a suitable least-effort integral in closed form which reproduced the differential equations as their Euler conditions. Euler conditions are first-order (necessary) conditions of a calculus of variations problem, see Intriligator (1971). This result by Volterra is further discussed in Part II, C. Further, Volterra was able to derive their Hamiltonian (again, see Intriligator (1971) for its definition) and interpret these potentials as 'ecological' potentials.

Since the earlier work by Lotka, Volterra, and others, the field has grown exponentially. Key contributions since then have been made by MacArthur (1965) and later by May. A good collection of essays showing the state of the art in contemporary mathematical ecology is the second edition of the book edited by May (1981). Of particular interest to economists and geographers in that collection may be the article by Colin Clark on the economics of renewable resource management.

2. Bifurcation

Consider a dynamical system of the form

$$\frac{\mathrm{d}}{\mathrm{d}t} x = F(x, \theta)$$

where x and F are n-dimensional vectors and θ is an m-dimensional vector of parameters. As θ changes, the phase plane also changes. Usually the change is continuous, but at certain bifurcation points the change in dynamic trajectories is abrupt. The simplest bifurcation is found in the simplest differential equation

$$\frac{dx}{dt} = ax$$

as a varies from $-\infty$ to $+\infty$. Negative a generates a set of negative exponential trajectories, whereas positive a depicts exponential growth. At zero the trajectories bifurcate as shown in Fig. I.1. A slightly more complicated example, found in Clark (1976), is the following

$$\frac{dx}{dt} = y$$

$$\frac{dy}{dt} = x^2 - y - a.$$

The equilibrium points are $y^* = 0$ and $x^* = \pm\sqrt{a}$. If a is negative there are no real valued equilibria. If a is positive there are two $[\sqrt{(a)}, 0]$ and $[-\sqrt{(a)}, 0]$. Linearizing around these points one obtains the matrix

$$A = \begin{bmatrix} 0 & 1 \\ \pm 2\sqrt{a} & -1 \end{bmatrix}$$

with eigenvalues λ^1 and λ^2 at $(\sqrt{a}, 0)$ and $(-\sqrt{a}, 0)$ such that

$$\lambda^1 = \frac{-1 \pm\sqrt{[1 + 8\sqrt{(a)}]}}{2} \qquad \lambda^2 = \frac{-1 \pm\sqrt{[1 - 8\sqrt{(a)}]}}{2}.$$

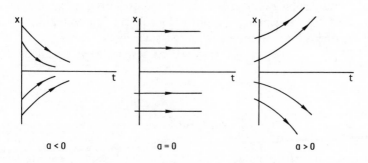

FIG. I.1. *The simplest bifurcation: the exponential function*

The first intersection of isoclines always implies a saddle, since $1 + 8\sqrt{a} > 0$. One eigenvalue is positive whereas the other is negative. However, in the second intersection $1 - 8\sqrt{a}$ could be positive, zero, or negative. At the point where it is zero ($a = 1/64$) the nature of the dynamic path changes. As a increases the system's trajectories are transformed from a stable node (λ^1, λ^2 negative, real, unequal) to a stable focus (λ^1, λ^2 complex, with negative real parts).

Another simple bifurcation is the one associated with the Volterra-Lotka system under limits to growth due to friction effects in the growth of x (or y)

$$\frac{dx}{dt} = x(a - by - ex)$$

$$\frac{dy}{dt} = y(cx - d).$$

At $e = 0$ the damped oscillatory motion (sink spiral) is transformed into a centre (orbital motion). For $e < 0$ the sink spiral becomes a source spiral.

3. The Van der Pol equation and the Hopf bifurcation

One of the best-known oscillatory patterns is depicted by the Van der Pol equation

$$\frac{d^2x}{dt^2} = -k(x^2 - b)\frac{dx}{dt} - x; \quad k > 0.$$

When $b < 0$ the coefficient $k(x^2 - b)$ of dx/dt is positive. This coefficient is the damping influence on the system, with the origin in this case being a stable focus. When b is positive, for small values of x relative to b, the damping is negative so that the origin is a spiralling source. Once $x^2 > b$ the damping is positive, and whatever the initial amplitude of the oscillations the system tends to a stable limit cycle.

The above system can be rewritten as a system of two equations

$$\frac{dx}{dt} = y$$

$$\frac{dy}{dt} = -k(x^2 - b)y - x.$$

Its phase portrait is shown in Fig. I.2. For some positive value of b the system switches to limit cycle behaviour, whereas for b positive and k

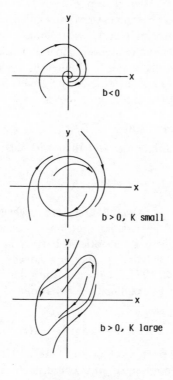

FIG. I.2. *The Van der Pol equation as a planar system*

large the limit cycle takes on a very distinct form. The bifurcation which occurs as b passes through the critical value zero transforms the origin from a stable focus to an unstable one surrounded by a stable limit cycle (Fig. I.2). This phenomenon, the birth of stable orbits out of a stable foci as a single parameter varies, is known as the Hopf bifurcation.

The Hopf theorem, discussed extensively in Marsden and McCracken (1976), Casti (1979), and others, shows the conditions under which the trajectories of the system

$$\frac{dx}{dt} = f(x, y, b)$$

$$\frac{dy}{dt} = g(x, y, b)$$

qualitatively change as b changes signs. An equilibrium at the origin will bifurcate into a stable limit cycle with radius proportional to b. The Hopf bifurcation theorem is applicable to n-dimensions (Cronin, 1977), but the assumptions made and the limited information obtained with regard to the stability properties severely restrain the use of the theorem for practical applications in higher dimensions.

4. The May–Li–Yorke chaos

Certain time-delay differential and first-order difference equations of the form

$$x(t+1) = F(x(t), a)$$

describe time-lags in the dynamics of a system, which produce in certain domains of values of the parameter seemingly stochastic as well as what is frequently referred to as 'chaotic' behaviour in x. This fixed-point algorithm has been analysed by May in a cascade of publications, for example May (1974, 1975, 1976, and for a survey 1979). May and others have extensively examined the behaviour of the simple iterative function

$$x(t+1) = a\,x(t)\,[1 - x(t)]$$

and slight variations of it, see May and Oster (1976). It must be noted that, although the above equation is one discrete time analogue to the continuous time logistic growth equation (dot indicating time derivative)

$$\dot{x} = ax\,(1 - x),$$

it does not depict in general logistic growth, but rather an oscillatory dynamic pattern. Equilibrium in this difference equation is obtained when $x(t+1) = x(t)$ at some time period t. This condition, plus the original difference equation plotted in the $x(t+1), x(t)$ space result in a phase portrait showing a hump intersected by the 45°-line (Fig. I.3).

At the equilibrium state the value of x remains constant: $x^* = (a-1)/a$, with a slope at the fixed point $s = 2 - a$ and a maximum at $a/4$; a cannot exceed 4 given that x cannot exceed 1. The equilibrium is stable as long as the slope at the fixed point lies between $+1$ and -1. This requires that $1 < a < 3$ (since $-1 < s < 1$). As a exceeds 3 the fixed point becomes unstable. When $a > 4$ the population becomes extinct.

For values of a greater than 3 the slope s steepens beyond -1. The equilibrium *is no longer a fixed value of x* but instead a repeated pattern

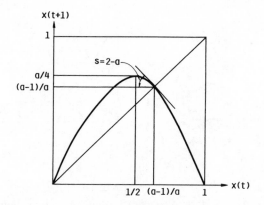

FIG. I.3. *The plotting of the function* $x(t + 1) = a\,x(t)\,[1 - x(t)]$

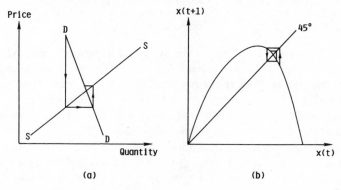

FIG. I.4. (a) *The cobweb and* (b) *May models*

such that at some future time period $t + k$ the value of $x(t + k)$ is equal
to the value of $x(t)$. Suppose that the value of $x(t)$ attains the same
magnitude two time-periods later so that $x(t + 2) = x(t)$. Then looking
at the 'time-period 2' function $x(t + 2) = F^{(2)}(x(t))$ the slope at the
fixed point (unstable equilibrium) is $s^{(2)} = [s^{(1)}]^2$. Positive slope there
implies two additional intersections of this function with the 45°-line
both stable. This depicts the fact that the dynamic trajectory is an
oscillation passing through these two equilibrium points in a pattern
repeated every second time-period (Fig. I.5).

This process gives rise to a pitchfork-type bifurcation phenomenon
so that within the domain $3 < a < 3.57$ there are $2k$, $4k$, $8k$, ... $2^n k$

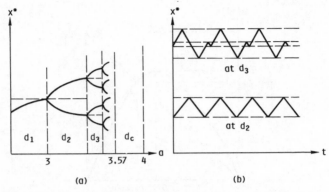

FIG. I.5. *Complex dynamic behaviour of the simple iterative model*
(a) In d_1 equilibrium value of x is constant; in d_2 the value of x is
repeated every second time-period; in d_3 there are two stable equilibrium patterns containing four points each approached asymptotically
every fourth time-period. (b) The patterns at d_2 and d_3 are shown near
their stable-limit cycle points, over time.

successive period-doubling stable cycles with periods (and repeated
points) $2, 4, 8, \ldots 2^n$ as a increases. Beyond this point of accumulation
of stable cycles lies the regime referred to as 'chaotic'. This regime
$(3.57 < a < 4)$ is composed of infinitely small intervals of a, each
corresponding to a stable cycle of period k and its cascade of (points)
period $2^n k$ (May 1979). First, all even-period cycles appear beyond the
initial value $a = 3.57$, in descending order; then (at $a = 3.67$), the first
odd-period cycle appears succeeded by all odd-period cycles in descending order. When the period-3 cycle appears (at $a = 3.82$) every other
integer- (odd or even) period cycle has already appeared; beyond this
value no periodic cycle occurs. This is Li and Yorke's (1975) contribution 'period three implies chaos'. Li and Yorke have shown this to
hold for a broader class of dynamic models. Since the original work by
May (to whom many attribute this model) and by Li–Yorke a large number of refinements of this turbulent behaviour have appeared that have
shifted the interest from its ecological to purely mathematical aspects.

The May model is very similar to the cobweb model in economics
(Fig. I.4(a)), where the relative slope of the demand and supply curves
determines the stability of the equilibrium. In this case (Fig. I.4(b)), the
demand curve is bent and the $45°$-line acts as the supply curve of the
economic model (with slope equal to one). An interesting application
of the May model in capital accumulation theory is that by Day (1982).

Wilson (1981) and his co-workers at Leeds have also used this model for simulating the behaviour of shopping activity in urban areas. Dendrinos (1984c) examines its use in urban dynamics.

Time-delay differential equations are capable of producing similar results. Consider the time-delay differential equation

$$\frac{\mathrm{d}x}{\mathrm{d}t} = -ax(t) + bx(t-T)\,[1 - x(t-T)^\alpha]$$

where T is the time lag. This particular equation, reported in May (1979), has been used to model population of baleen whales. It possesses the non-zero equilibrium

$$x^* = [1 - a/b]^{1/\alpha}$$

where $a/b > 1$ is the ratio of per capita death to birth-rates. This equation has been shown to possess chaotic properties. A vast array of time-delay models were originally examined by Volterra.

It must be noted that the above phenomena are not stochastic but deterministic. The May model was presented to make the point that it is not necessary to introduce randomness into non-linear model-building to simulate non-stable oscillatory motions. However, these results can be replicated and they are not haphazard. The dynamics exhibit pseudo-random behaviour.

5. Structural stability and elementary catastrophe theory

In this book, catastrophe theory is not used directly in the exposition of the main topics. Reference to it is made, however, to indicate possible extensions of the models presented here along its lines. Thus, no formal introduction to the theory is provided here. The interested reader is directed to either the original work by Thom (1975), or its subsequent introductions by Zeeman (1977), Amson (1975), Poston and Stewart (1978), Woodcock and Poston (1974), Saunders (1980), Casti (1982), and Gilmore (1981). The pioneer in applying catastrophe theory to urban analysis has been John Amson (1972, 1973). His were the earliest papers that brought catastrophe theory to the attention of urban researchers. However, his very innovative line of research has not been further developed in the last ten years. For a survey of earlier attempts to use catastrophe theory in urban, regional, transportation research the reader is directed to Wilson (1981) and Dendrinos (1980a). Additional work in applying catastrophe theory to urban and regional systems has been that by Mees (1975), Puu (1979) drawing from earlier work by Beckmann (1952) on continuous transportation flow fields; and by Casetti (1981), Nijkamp (1982), Dendrinos (1976, 1978), Orishimo (1980), and others.

Briefly, catastrophe theory addresses itself to the properties of structural stability underlying systems governed by potentials. When these potentials are non-linear, then through appropriate co-ordinate transformations one can derive certain singularities which correspond to the family of functions associated with the original potentials. Catastrophe theory analyses the behaviour of the transformed system at the neighbourhood of these singularities. Thom's classification theory identifies the types of singularities expected of the transformed system (the canonical form) on the basis of its number of state variables and necessary (co-ordinate transformed) parameters along which the singularity(ies) is(are) recorded. The steps covering the necessary co-ordinate transformations from the original system to the transformed one, and the necessary conditions to be satisfied by the original system's potential in order to give rise to particular catastrophes (discontinuities in canonical form) are given by Zeeman (1977), Poston and Stewart (1978) and Casti (1982) among others. These steps have been followed by Dendrinos (1984b) in deriving the potential type governing the cusp catastrophe underlying the dynamics of nine US regions, recorded in Dendrinos (1984a).

An important use one can make of the canonical form of the various catastrophes is through the combination of a fast motion underlying changes in the state variable(s) and a slow motion underlying changes in the parameter(s) or 'control variable(s)'. The original work was provided by Zeeman (1977). As the subject of slow and fast motion is central to this book the Zeeman model is discussed in Appendix II.

C. CONCLUSIONS

Some key models of dynamic stability and bifurcation were reviewed as the key methodological tools to be employed in the construction of an urban ecological theory of evolution. The features of the eigenvalues of the characteristic polynomial of the linearized system from the original system of differential equations is the determinant of local dynamic stability. Bifurcation is the change of the nature of the dynamic equilibria locally, due to infinitesimal changes of key model parameters. Urban development is here associated with a particular path, in turn associated with a specific dynamic equilibrium; whereas urban evolutionary events occur when the nature of the dynamic equilibrium changes due to smooth change in key parameter(s). These bifurcations are recorded along isoclines in the phase portrait of a dynamic system.

Attention was paid to a particular model, developed by May; the model generates turbulent behaviour out of very simple dynamic specifications in difference and certain time-delay differential equations. This particular model is of interest because it demonstrates that in nature seemingly disordered (turbulent) complex processes can be produced by orderly, smooth, and infinitesimal changes in key parameters of very simple dynamic systems. It demonstrates that one need not resort to complex models to simulate complexity. Some interesting extensions of this line of research is presented in the work by M. Feigenbaum (1980) which focuses, among other items, on the Duffing equation. Feigenbaum finds universal principles governing certain iterative processes (the difference and differential equations discussed earlier merely being part of them) which are governed by particular bifurcations on their way to chaotic behaviour, independent of the specific form of the original system. These developments represent only one line of work in the quickly expanding field of bifurcation theory. The reader is directed to Gurel and Rossler (1979) for a collection of contributions to the theory and its applications in a number of disciplines.

Part II.

URBAN ECOLOGY: INTER-URBAN DYNAMICS

A. INTRODUCTION

A short list of some recent as well as long-standing questions, some related and others quite diverse in nature, is provided below. Mathematical ecology seems to be capable of providing a sufficiently broad framework to accomodate these classes of problems, when suitably modified for an urban context. The basic ingredient it supplies is a genuinely dynamic framework within which an array of interesting urban events falls.

Any assembly of intereacting cities in a region or a nation poses a host of questions. Why are there no more (or less) cities within a particular region at a particular time-period? Why are there relatively small regions containing a relatively large number of cities (the north-eastern seaboard of the US for example); whereas in other cases a small number of cities is found in a relatively large area (the plains region of the US)? How is their number changing over time? Why do cities appear or disappear suddenly at particular locations at certain points in time? Why is a city's population no greater (or less) than its current level? Why does a city's population level change in certain instances gradually, whereas in other cases it follows quite violent outbursts over short time-periods?

Is the decline of one city necessary for the growth of another and vice versa? Is this growth/decline phenomenon necessary for the welfare of a nation at large? Why do some cities grow simultaneously, whereas others decline simultaneously, or remain at a steady state? Is there a nation-wide pattern which governs the dynamics of all cities at all time-periods, or are there regional patterns? And over what variables are such patterns defined and what form do they have? How stable over time are these patterns?

What constitutes 'neighbouring' or 'similar' cities? Along what dimensions can one classify certain cities as belonging to a local group? Is physical location or age important for such clustering? How are various environment changes in the region or the nation absorbed by the urban system in the short and long run? Similar questions one can ask for communities within cities.

Some of these and related questions have in the past been addressed by urban and regional location theory, central place theory, urban and regional economics. In contributions to *Geographical Analysis* (1983) the question is brought up, rekindled by Y. Papageorgiou (1982), whether existing theories provide satisfactory answers to such questions. Although researchers' views differ, it seems that all contributors to that discussion more or less agree that our understanding of urban phenomena, urban form, its structure, and processes of change leaves room for improvement.

A great deal of attention has been directed toward urban economic analysis. Competitive equilibrium economics, however, presents a rather restrictive manner in which to examine urban systems. This line of research is vulnerable on two counts: first, dynamic adjustments are not explicitly dealt with, especially those that are associated with highly non-linear and bifurcating behaviour. Under these circumstances the conditions for uniqueness break down. Second, empirical work has not been abundant in documenting a merely urban economic-based theory. Some of these criticisms are not only applicable to urban and regional economics, but also to general economic theory, Hayek (1975). Attempts to address these issues are found in Szego (1982) and Smale (1979).

In a separate effort, Samuelson (1971), recognizing the attractive elements of mathematical ecology, has attempted to establish a unified economic–ecological theory. However, the point has been made in the past that economic theory is only a part of ecological theory, since 'economic competition is only a special form of the more general phenomenon of biological competition' (Lotka, 1932).

The potential of using the formalism of mathematical ecology in urban analysis has been advocated by a number of researchers in the field. In the last ten years or so an increasing quantity of literature is appearing on this topic. Among the first recorded attempts in non-linear dynamic urban mathematical modelling were these by P. Allen *et al.* (1978) and Wilson (1981) along large-scale modelling lines. Use of a Volterra–Lotka formalism has been made by Curry (1981) in the case of occupations competing for labour in spatially structured labour markets; and by Sonis (1983) in modelling geographical innovation-diffusion processes. In terms of an explicit urban ecological theory and problem-specific modelling conducive to analytical treatment, the earliest efforts were those by Dendrinos (1979) and Dendrinos and Mullally (1982a). An extension of the latter line of work is the subject of this book.

Starting in the mid 1970s, a group of researchers at the University of Brussels produced a number of urban models which one could classify as ecological. The group was centred around the pioneer in the field of non-linear dynamics and bifurcation theory in physical chemistry, Ilya Prigogine. Their efforts, as shown in the work by Allen *et al.* (1978) covered both inter- and intra-urban dynamics. Dendrinos (1980a) and Wilson (1981) provide a comprehensive review of their work.

Their emphasis was not so much to link general ecology to urban ecology as a quest for bifurcation phenomena and stochasticity. Although their large-scale dynamical systems are attractive, since they can be thought of as tactical models and thus more closely replicating quite complicated urban interactions, they have the drawback that they lack analytical solution. As a result, it is not clear what these models produce qualitatively at each time-period, in terms of dynamic equilibria. Further, because of the exogenously introduced fluctuations in their model it is not computationally feasible to identify precisely possible bifurcations and the critical points where such bifurcations may occur. More attractive is the work by Allen and Sanglier (1981) in attempting to reformulate central place theory in a dynamic framework.

Wilson and his co-workers at Leeds have produced an array of publications extending their spatial interaction models using catastrophe theory (Wilson, 1981). Their suggestions span both residential and retail service location modelling, although their most prominent work is the extension of an earlier retail trade model by Harris (1965). Contrary to the Allen models elements of bifurcating behaviour can be computationally captured in the Wilson models when urban zones are viewed in isolation (Harris and Wilson, 1978). The Wilson work lends itself to the application of May's iterative (turbulent behaviour) model. However, due to the dimensionality of the Wilson model, its outcome for any particular retail zone is not the deterministic pseudo-random behaviour found in the May model. The precise nature of the dynamic is unknown. Clarke and Wilson (1983) can only characterize it as either stable, unstable, or 'periodic'.

So far, both of these lines of work have remained at the computer simulation level. Clearly, empirical verification is needed to test them. Validation of such models will prove that indeed non-linearities of the kind suggested are present in the particular urban systems analysed, which Wilson classifies as belonging to a 'mesoscale'. Possible extensions of these models will make them more problem specific, i.e. capable of addressing a particular event or phenomenon rather than merely provide the framework for a number of problems to be analysed. One would be looking for a more focused tactical model if one were to be policy oriented. However, how one can window into these models at this stage is an open and interesting research question.

In his book, Wilson (1981) presents an overview of mathematical ecology and the Volterra–Lotka formalism specifically; although he does not enter into details he mentions the work by May on complexity versus stability and on the complex behaviour of simple dynamical models. He hints that the potential for urban analysis of mathematical ecology is significant.

In summary: a number of questions in dynamic urban theory are not yet fully answered. Mathematical ecology seems to provide a broad theoretical framework for the construction of urban dynamic models, as exemplified by a number of recent contributions.

B. EQUIVALENCES BETWEEN GENERAL ECOLOGY AND URBAN ECOLOGY: TOWARDS A 'NEW URBAN ECOLOGICAL' THEORY

Next, certain substantive and methodological similarities will be drawn between general ecology and urban ecology. Mention of certain germane differences will also be made. Key methodological similarities will be used to provide the basis of the inter- and intra-urban ecological theory and modelling proposed. Other substantive similarities or dissimilarities will be mentioned but not elaborated; instead they are left to the interested reader to ponder.

Urban ecology has a long history, going back to the work by Hoyt (1933) and the Chicago School. That work, however, was not quantitative in nature, but rather descriptive and qualitative, bearing little connection to the theory of mathematical ecology and its emphasis on stability properties of dynamically interacting species. Although the early urban ecology did provide some interesting insights into intra-urban spatial segregation of various socio-economic groups, it did not follow the methodological and substantive developments in general ecology over the past fifty years. Some recent work to reformalize urban ecology has been that by Berry and Kasarda (1977). Our work here can be thought of as descending from the earlier work by the Chicago School in view of the significant developments made since both in urban economics and urban systems theory, as well as mathematical ecology.

It is useful to view each city as a distinct population-type consisting of a number of individuals at any time-period. Then, one can consider as many populations (or 'species' in the ecological literature — equivalent only so far as the method is concerned) within a nation or a region as there are cities. In this framework, the correspondence with biological species does not go beyond mere methodological similarities. General ecology recognizes that within a particular environment there is a community of species interacting with one another. So are systems of cities within a region or a nation; and so are various neighbourhoods with cities. In general ecology there are particular types of associations among species: symbiotic, predatory, competitive, commensal, amensal, and isolative. They are based on merely formal inter-species attraction or repulsion (antagonistic) interdependencies. In basic mathematical ecology these interactions are modelled with no reference to the biology of the species. The thesis of this book is that there are equivalent associations among metropolitan areas constituting the urban sector of a nation, and among neighbourhoods within cities.

These interactions are manifested in a variety of forms: cities import from and/or export to other cities, input/output commodities, finance capital, population (labour). As a result of such exchanges, while some cities expand others shrink. At the intra-urban level, there is a flow of workers, shoppers, residents, land values, commodities, etc., from one zone to another. As particular land uses appear at particular locations and then grow in density, others or similar uses decline and disappear from other zones. These patterns present spatial as well as temporal regularities over different time-scales. Ecological interactions are ubiquitous among and within metropolitan settings.

Inter-species attraction/repulsion and intra-species affinity/resistance in general ecology can be viewed as the main ingredient within and among cities and neighbourhoods interaction. This equivalence is the major motivating factor in establishing methodological links between urban and general ecology. They are the main subject of this book and are elaborated in Sections C-G. Various kinds of connectance among cities are at the centre of urban landscapes, either geographic or economic. A community of cities interaction matrix describes the stability properties of the different locales in these landscapes. These topics constitute the subject of most of Parts II and III in their respective framework of inter- and intra-urban dynamics.

The mathematical ecology formalism can provide some guidance on how one may be able to address urban dynamics. It will be shown in this Part that predatory dynamics can simulate inter-urban linkages; whereas, in the next Part it will be demonstrated that competitive and predatory dynamics can provide the patterns underlying neighbourhood composition. One may find that beyond such purely methodological equivalences, there are certain substantive linkages between urban and general ecology. Speciation and ecological diversity may provide some insights into the way the problems of urban industrial specialization, introduction of new towns, and formation of urban hierarchies are stated. Rain forest ecology may provide hints into the abstract mechanisms underlying the density-of-cities dynamic in the north-eastern seaboard of the US. In general ecology, rain forests are associated with relatively high density (variety) of species in space, and strong interactions. Similar conditions may characterize this particular region of the US. Two other ecological notions, niche and patchiness, seem to be potentially very insightful in the field of urban ecology. They will be reviewed in sequence next, although they will not be the subject of analysis here. Niche (Hutchinson, 1978) is the set of points in the abstract space defined over key attributes describing the habitat (locationally defined) of species. Population abundance of other cities can be considered part of a metropolitan area's niche. Niche size is partly defined as the space over which a city extends its influence. Niche size, niche overlap, and niche dynamics for individual cities at the inter-urban level point to locational factors underlying city existence at a particular point in a region. Spatial competition for primary resources, capital, labour, population, and output markets determine at any given point in time the niche size and its dynamics for a particular city within a community of cities. In general ecology, influence is a decreasing function of distance. So is influence of cities or neighbourhoods or land uses in the field of urban ecology.

Spacing of individuals (groups) belonging to a particular species, i.e. territoriality, is seen in general ecology as obeying two time-scales: centre of the territory is chosen so that in a first optimization process maximum utilization of the spatial influence is achieved. Then size of the territory is determined by a second optimization process where a minimum threshold required for survival is obtained. Spacing of cities, i.e. their specific point location in the national space can be viewed as the slow dynamic involved in the first optimization function of ecological habitat. Cities appear at (or disappear from) specific points in the national space and grow/decline in response to locational advantages differentially enjoyed at these points and their neighbourhood. Over shorter time-spans, each city behaves as if it were to extend its influence over the minimum space (market area) required to support its population at a given reward level. So the slow inter-urban dynamic is change in population; the fast inter-urban dynamic is the extent of the market, i.e. the efficient territorial extension over space through appropriate trading patterns.

Since urban areas do not contain homogeneous populations, contrary to ecological niches, niche overlap is a rule in urban ecology. As different kinds of consumers, firms, and governments operate within a metropolitan area, the influence patterns are not identical. This is one reason why the Christaller construct in market area analysis of locational economics is not satisfactory. Market areas of cities cannot be clearly delineated by strict limits. The widespread phenomenon of cities annexing fringe territory is evidence of minimum territory adjustment necessary for the efficient serving of a city's population. This, in connection with the decentralization event of residential and industrial activity within metropolitan areas, can be viewed in combination as slow marginal adjustments of the centre of the city in the national space.

Some aspects of spatial patchiness, spatial patch dynamics and their qualitative properties are studied in the intra-urban portion of this book. Particularly, the incidence of slum formation and slum expansion dynamics identify processes analogous to patch dynamics in general ecology. At the inter-urban level, patchiness is more difficult to define and detect. One might produce a typology of cities, for example the category 'cities in distress' according to various socio-economic indicators, and try to identify their location in the national space. In the popular press the north-eastern and north-central regions of the US are identified as containing such cities, much more in proportion than the southern and western regions. Then one might view distress as patchiness being propagated. Although such research might be promising, it will not be developed here any further. Curry (1981) discussed more extensively the use of patchiness in labour occupation dynamics.

There are rules in general ecology of optimum and equilibrium community composition (i.e. optimum and equilibrium number of species, as well as optimum/equilibrium population level within each species). There are attempts to define the rules governing, in an equivalent manner, the optimum/equilibrium number of towns in a region/nation, and the optimum/equilibrium population size of each city. A notable difference between general and urban ecology at the inter-urban level is the sense in which the term 'management' is used: optimum pest control, maximum yield, etc., management is external in the field of general ecology, whereas management is internal in urban ecology. This difference may lessen at the intra-urban level when coupled with foresight in the behaviour of the various consumers, producers, and government agents. At this level management may be feasible, but at the inter-urban level management may not. Some of these topics on optimality particularly when viewed in a relative growth framework within a policy-making context will be addressed in Section I of Part II and Part IV.

In general ecology there are species, genera, families, orders, etc. In an analogical manner one can consider cities to differ taxonomically because their industrial bases differ. In the US the Standard Industrial Classification Code (SIC) classifies various producing units on the basis of their output according to a taxonomy extended over four digits of detail. A city's diversity of output production crosses over these SIC boundaries. Thus cities do not belong exclusively to one category, although for certain industrially specialized cities one industry dominates all others. Interdependencies among the various industries of a city or region with other cities and regions is the subject of interregional input–output studies (Isard, 1975). Locational comparative advantages underlie the presence of particular industries at particular locales at specific time-periods and efficiency in the production and distribution of input and output commodities and production resources underlie locational interdependencies. All this is well discussed in conventional regional science literature, and it seems that conventional ecology could gain somewhat by reviewing this literature.

Taxonomic breakdowns in urban ecological theory produce a hierarchy of urban structure quite distinct from the traditional Christaller–Lösch type of central place theory. Ecological hierarchy follows the industrial classification breakdown, so that evolutionary change in industrial production is directly linked with dynamic changes in the urban hierarchy. Urban hierarchy formation, its underlying dynamics, stability and evolution are topics to be addressed in (Part II, H) and ecological theory can be of considerable assistance.

However, along with the previously listed methodological and potentially substantive similarities there are significant substantive and methodological differences as well. They provide interest in an effort to derive an urban ecology as a branch of general ecology.

From a substantive viewpoint, in contrast to general ecology where different communities consist of different animal or plant species, cities are inhabited by human population, by different firms, and by various types of governing bodies. Classification of different towns as different populations may be taxonomic with respect to individuals, firms, or governments they contain, but membership commutes. Individuals can move to different towns; firms may alter their output; governments may change their functions. In particular, consumers' behaviour may be the outcome of different income levels, preference functions, race, age, education, and other socio-economic characteristics. Similarly, there are attributes along which the behaviour of different firms and governments can be recorded. Within each of these clubs, there could still be variability in behaviour. Were individual variability in behaviour within a group significant, then micro-behaviour based models reproducing aggregate group behaviour would be called for. The extent to which this is necessary in urban dynamics is analysed in Part III, H. One would expect within species variability in non-human ecology to be much more limited. We will not address any further the substantive differences between human communities and other ecological communities. In this book we will treat population dynamics in an abstract manner, where the *interdependencies among and within populations are removed from the specific biology, sociology, or economy of these populations*.

From a methodological standpoint, attention will be drawn to two key differences between urban and general ecology: that of demand-supply interations; and absolute/relative growth. They will be discussed briefly in turn.

In both inter- and intra-urban dynamics populations interact under the influence of two functions: an internally (within group) generated response function to a varying environment, i.e. a demand function; and an externally (outside the group) generated response due to inter-group interaction, i.e. a supply function. In general ecology, according to the Volterra–Lotka formalism, a single species growth is modelled by one kinetic equation, and n-species interactions are contained in an n-equations model. In urban ecology, a single population model requires two kinetic equations and an n-population model contains $2n$ differential equations. In the case of inter-urban dynamics, the single open city dynamic model contains two differential equations, depicting demand for and supply of urban population based on different levels of some factor reward. From a methodological standpoint, the single-city dynamic model corresponds to the two species predator–prey ecological model (see Section 3, in this Part). If capital is to enter the analysis, then the single-city model will consist of three kinetic equations (a problem addressed in Section G of this Part).

The second major difference between urban and general mathematical ecology is the use of *relative* v. *absolute* growth models. Since relative growth models are the focus in this book few remarks will be made here as an introduction to the subject of relative growth. Clearly, relative and absolute growth depict different processes at work. Relative growth is tied to elasticities of local growth with respect to growth-rate of a broader entity (environment) over which population (or any other variable) is normalized. Consequently, it depends on relative distribution of endowments (comparative advantages) to the various locations in the environment. From a local standpoint, these differentials are more important than absolute levels in determining growth/decline possibilities. Cities (i.e. locales) compete for a portion of a nation's resource, population (labour), by being able to offer a factor reward level (income) relative to other locales. Further, the competitive or predatory connections among different localities can be more vividly captured through relative growth models. This makes more sense in the urban context, where (as already mentioned) membership by the population among different cities commutes.

In summary: the foundation of a 'new urban ecological' theory has been laid down. Central to this urban mathematical ecology modelling is the possibility to incorporate all ecological associations within and among urban settings. The six basic ecological associations, which underlie the dynamic non-linear interdependencies among populations in general mathematical ecology, can now be transferred to urban dynamical interactions. Inter- and intra-urban interdependencies are thus viewed as competitive, predatory, etc. This is the major methodological similarity linking urban and general ecology. It allows for population interactions to be viewed removed from their particular sociology, economy, or biology; instead it calls for a general methodological framework to be adopted.

Substantive similarities were mentioned between urban and general mathematical ecology; in particular niche, niche overlap, and niche dynamics; patchiness and patch dynamics; taxonomic and hierarchical decomposition and dynamics. Certain key substantive and methodological dissimilarities were discussed, too. Specifically, the demand–supply components missing in multi-species ecological interactions, as well as relative growth dynamics, mostly absent from general ecology, were identified as key ingredients of an urban mathematical framework.

C. INTER-URBAN MATHEMATICAL ECOLOGY

In this Section the main theoretical framework and models for inter-urban dynamics are provided. In Section C.1 the simple logistic growth model and its theoretical base are presented. In Section C.2 the economic predecessor of the urban Volterra–Lotka model is discussed. In Section C.3 the basic inter-urban single-city Volterra–Lotka model is outlined. Finally, in Section C.4 a price–quantity version of the basic Volterra–Lotka model is supplied. Inter-urban dynamics, it can be easily argued, consists of very complex processes. The thesis of this Section is that, such complexity notwithstanding, a city's dynamic is simple when appropriately defined at the macroscopic level.

1. Single-city aggregate dynamics; no reward function

This particular abstraction of a closed city (isolated urban species) is presented primarily to set the stage for the more elaborate urban models to follow. Its purpose is mostly expository in that it is to introduce the basic elements involved in urban ecology. Following the standard model from general ecology the city's behaviour is modelled in a dynamic framework. An ordinary differential equation, with no time-lag, is proposed to describe the aggregate population x of a given city at a given time-period t

$$\frac{dx(t)}{dt} = f(x(t))$$

so that growth (or decline) is a continuous function of time. There are no interactions with other towns in this isolated city with its rate of population change depending solely upon its current level. Two particular specifications of the above formulation have been widely used in a variety of fields. One is the Malthusian type

$$\frac{dx}{dt} = \alpha x \rightarrow x(t) = x_o \exp(\alpha t)$$

with constant exponential growth (decline) rate α (the difference between birth- and death-rates), where x_o is the original perturbation (the initial population at time $t = 0$). At the neighbourhood of $\alpha = 0$ (the separatrix), the trajectory of x bifurcates from positive to negative exponential. The other is the logistic equation of the Verhulst–Pearl type where α is itself a linear function of x

$$\frac{dx}{dt} = x(\alpha - \beta x) = \alpha x(1 - \frac{\beta}{\alpha} x)$$

where α is the intrinsic growth (decline) rate and α/β is a carrying capacity (limit) imposed upon the species by the environment and/or its internal interactions.

Volterra (1939) derived the potential which gives rise to the Verhulst-Pearl equation. If by X one designates the total quantity of life over a time-horizon t

$$X(t) = \int_0^t x(t)dt$$

and by $F(t)$ the integrand

$$F(t) = m_1 \times \ln x + m_2 (\alpha - \beta x) \ln (\alpha - \beta x) + kX$$

where m_1, m_2, k appropriate non-negative numbers, then the least effort integral P

$$P(t) = \int_0^t F(t)dt$$

if minimized by suitable variation of X over the time-interval t produces the Verhulst–Pearl equation as its Euler condition. The proof is found in Appendix III.

The justification for using as the building block of urban dynamics the Verhulst–Pearl equation is twofold: it is the simplest differential equation which describes (without necessarily explaining) certain growth/decline patterns. Particularly, it describes observed dynamical paths of metropolitan populations with exponential growth or decline near their original perturbation (starting-points); and it replicates through its expected stability properties the behaviour of urban populations near their saturation levels. In short, it is the simplest model containing negative density dependence interaction. Further, it is the first two terms in a power series expansion of a general growth model.

One must accept under the above specifications that the outside world and its interactions with the city remain constant over time, in this case, isolation. Evolutionary changes do not occur in the closed city, only development. Malthusian and/or equations of the Verhulst–Pearl type.cannot hold true indefinitely but only for limited time-horizons. Eventually, the population accumulation will exhaust the available resources. The city will experience fatigue. Thus, the population may settle down to some steady state over certain time-periods (with or without fluctuations) but eventually it will decline until the resources are renewed (if ever). The system will shift to a different kinetic condition. As seen later, this basic proposition holds true in even more complicated formulations of the urban ecological model. In the simple logistic growth model, there is an inference of some interaction between resources and consumers in its parameters. For reasons of reduced dimensionality they are not made explicit but only approximated (Schaffer, 1981).

2. *Economics of single-city dynamics with reward function*

First, the conventional urban economics model will be presented in a dynamic framework. Then, the urban ecological model will be outlined.

Traditional urban mathematical economics (Alonso, 1964, and many others since) describe individual behaviour in terms of maximizing a utility function subject to some exogenously fixed income (money and/or time) constraints along the lines of conventional mathematical micro-economics of consumer behaviour. The arguments of the utility function describing a typical resident of a town contains as arguments commodities locally consumed.

Cities are perceived in either a closed or open framework. In the first case the total resident population is fixed and the prevailing utility level, uniform for all at equilibrium, is endogenously derived; whereas, in the second case the utility level is fixed and the equilibrium population of the city is endogenously derived. The basic model is a static competitive (in an economic sense) equilbrium one. The theoretical background of this model can be found in Henderson (1977) and Wheaton (1974).

The implicit aggregate city dynamics of this process are depicted in Fig. II.1, from Dendrinos (1980b) (see Appendix IV). The strictly convex curve U^* depicts the maximum utility level attainable in a particular city at a particular size by a typical urban resident. The horizontal line at $\bar{U}$ depicts the infinitely elastic supply of labour (population) curve when the prevailing background national average utility level is $\bar{U}$. U^* is interpreted as the demand for labour (population) by the particular city from the rest of the nation. Point x_1, is an unstable equilibrium, leading to city extinction if the original perturbation is below level x_1, whereas x_2 is a stable one.

When the national landscape is homogeneous then all cities at equilibrium are identical in size at $(\bar{U}, x_2)$, or they become extinct, depending on their original position. In a more realistic framework, the

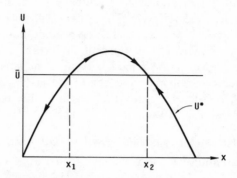

FIG. II.1. *The dynamics of an open city: fixed background utility level,
$\bar{U}$, and strictly convex equilibrium utility, U^**

national landscape is not homogeneous. Consumers and producers have
preferences over this heterogeneity, as well as over the (relative or
absolute) size of the cities. The latter has not been incorporated into
urban mathematical economics.

Part of the economists' omission can be relaxed by introducing
appropriate non-linearities in city size–utility interaction. A way to do
so is to introduce city size directly into the utility function of a typical
resident of a town. The end-result may be a two-hump equilibrium
utility level curve, U^*, like the one shown in Fig. II.2. Points x_2 and x_4

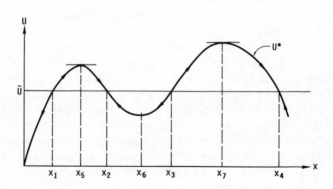

FIG. II.2. *Multiple maxima, single city dynamics*
Size is an argument in the utility function. $\bar{U}$ is the nation-wide prevailing utility level; x_1, x_3 are unstable sizes, whereas x_2, x_4 are stable sizes.

designate stable equilibria, whereas x_1 and x_3 are unstable. Any perturbation off the stable points will result in a fast size and utility level adjustment toward the nearest fast equilibrium.

It is of interest to study the structural stability aspects of this model. As any model parameter (say the price of a commodity in the local bundle, or an exogenous to the city price level) changes, the equilibrium city size may undergo drastic shifts, as shown in Fig. II.3. A price level, c, is continuously decreasing; as a result U^* (or $\bar{U}$) shifts. At either level c_1 or c_2 there is sudden change in the equilbrium city size, as size (x_5, x_6, x_7) thresholds are crossed. Sudden (fast) movement, associated with growth/decline, to an alternative (but stable) city size could result. Some unstable point could also be reached which could entail extinction or sustained explosive growth.

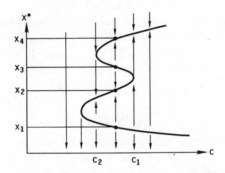

FIG. II.3. *The slow and fast movement of urban population*
The size x adjusts as the parameter c changes: movement in c corresponds to either shifts in $\bar{U}$ or U^*.

There are two difficulties associated with this model. One surrounds the motion of the fast city size adjustment: it is of a nodal type, and does not allow for oscillatory movement. Later in this Part extensive empirical evidence will be supplied to demonstrate that cycles are a ubiquitous phenomenon of aggregate urban dynamics. The second involves testing of the model. Utility is a non-observable (or recorded) quantity, and thus only indirect tests can be carried out regarding its effect on city size. A way out of the second predicament is to employ income counts, a surrogate for utility. The two are related so that higher utility levels always correspond to higher real incomes. Oscillations in one imply oscillations in the other. Limited time-series on income are available at the SMSA level from census sources.

But to address the first difficulty (lack of oscillations) using urban mathematical economic models seems to be much more challenging. No evidence has been supplied to demonstrate convincingly that urban economic models are capable of capturing rather simple aggregate urban dynamic patterns. Since the focus here is not only to set up models that would capture the essence of urban dynamic patterns recorded, but to do so in a parsimonious manner, an alternative approach must be adopted. We are now set to address the original proposition: the urban macro-behaviour is simple, in spite of its internal complexity.

3. The basic urban ecological model

Let the population of a town i be X_i and its factor reward (income) Y_i, whereas the environment of the town is taken to be the nation with population X and average prevailing factor reward Y. Then if we normalize with respect to that national count, the urban relative population and factor reward are $x_i = X_i/X$ and $y_i = Y_i/Y$ respectively.

Assume that relative population size and factor reward changes are simultaneously defined by the set of ordinary differential equations:

$$\dot{x} = f_1(x,y)$$

$$\dot{y} = f_2(x,y)$$

where dot stands for time derivative and y is the average intra-urban reward level at time t, and where the subscript i has been dropped for simplicity. Action is continuous, with no time-lags (same time-period adjustment of x with regard to y), and it does not have foresight built in at either end. Extensions if needed along these lines are left to the interested reader. The aim here is to outline the basic qualitative properties of the above dynamic model under particular specifications.

Two basic interdependencies are involved in the above formulation: first, the interaction between relative population and relative factor reward; second, the interaction between a single city and the national economy. The latter is depicted by the normalization of the urban population and factor reward levels with regard to the total national population and the average prevailing nation-wide factor reward. A particular specification of the above formulation is an exponentially fast adjustment to excess demand/supply conditions. The original system then obtains the form

$$\dot{x} = x\, F_1(x,y)$$

$$\dot{y} = y\, F_2(x,y)$$

where F_1, F_2 depend on the relative position the city occupies in the national economy.

The simplest specification of the proposed system of simultaneous differential equations in population and reward functions with exponentially fast adjustments to excess demand and supply conditions is the following version of the dissipative model

$$f = \dot{x} = x(a_1 + a_{11}x + a_{12}y)$$
$$g = \dot{y} = y(a_2 + a_{21}x + a_{22}y)$$

with $a_{11}x$ and $a_{22}y$ being the terms responsible for the dissipative motion. It involves linear demand and supply functions. Negative a_{11} implies the presence of net friction due to externalities of population agglomerations (congestion, density, pollution, etc., minus positive agglomeration economies); whereas negative a_{22} indicates net diseconomies in the income accumulation process (a highly unlikely event in urban ecology). On the other hand positive a_{11} and a_{22} imply net positive economies of agglomeration in population and reward accumulations. Thus, relative population and income are assumed to increase/decrease exponentially according to a modified Verhulst–Pearl equation.

Of particular interest is the behaviour of the above system in the neighbourhood of critical points x^*, y^*, where $\dot{x} = \dot{y} = 0$. The stability properties of this system have been widely discussed in the ecological and mathematical literature (Pavlidis (1973), Hirsch and Smale (1974), May (1973), etc.) and only the main points will be presented here. All depends upon the urban Jacobian matrix

$$A = \begin{bmatrix} \alpha_{11} = \dfrac{\partial f}{\partial x} \Big|_{x^*} & \alpha_{12} = \dfrac{\partial g}{\partial x} \Big|_{x^*} \\[2ex] \alpha_{21} = \dfrac{\partial f}{\partial y} \Big|_{y^*} & \alpha_{22} = \dfrac{\partial g}{\partial y} \Big|_{y^*} \end{bmatrix}$$

of the linearized system. The eigenvalues λ_1 and λ_2 of the characteristic polynomial of the linearized system

$$\lambda^2 - (\alpha_{11} + \alpha_{22})\lambda - \alpha_{12}\alpha_{21} + \alpha_{11}\alpha_{22} = 0$$

describe its local stability properties. The sign of the real parts of the two eigenvalues defines exponential growth/decline; whereas the square root term (depending on whether it is real or imaginary) determines the lack or existence of oscillatory motion. Imaginary roots imply oscillation. Specifically each and both of

$$f_x + f_y = \alpha_{11} + \alpha_{22} < 0$$

$$f_x g_y + g_x f_y = \alpha_{11} \cdot \alpha_{21} > 0$$

are the necessary and sufficient conditions for stability of the equilibrium. Oscillation depends upon the sign of the expression

$$(f_x + g_y)^2 - 4(f_x g_y - g_x f_y) \gtrless 0.$$

Nodes are obtained when the above is zero. Negativity implies oscillatory damping motion.

4. *Price-quantity functions and the Volterra-Lotka formalism*

A digression is made to point out certain interesting features of the above model, before discussing in more detail the urban ecological model of relative growth. To economists the structure of the Volterra–Lotka model must be of particular interest. Of course, in the above system F_1 and F_2 are the excess demand for and supply of relative population in the city in question, with reference to the national economy. Each isocline identifies conditions where excess is zero. At equilibrium both are zero.

Steady state conditions in the case of two-species population interactions is exactly the same as one-species, one-resource demand–supply equilibrium found in micro-economics, or price–quantity one-commodity interaction. Downward sloping demand curve and upward sloping supply curve imply that $\alpha_{12}/\alpha_{11} > 0$ and $-\alpha_{22}/\alpha_{21} > 0$ in the above system. However, this is not by itself, as was shown, a sufficient condition for stability.

Justification for an exponentially fast adjustment in excess demand–supply conditions can be drawn from two sources. Either by empirical evidence and testing, the basic motivation of the present work; or by behavioural assumptions postulating the existence of a particular least-effort integral (utility or profit function) giving rise to these excess quantity functions in a system resulting from the two first-order conditions. When the n-populations urban ecological model will be presented, .a few references will be made as to its consequence for a general equilibrium economy. From an ecological standpoint it is of interest to note that inter-species interactions can be viewed as demand for and supply of various species functions (Rapport and Turner, 1977).

D. INTER-URBAN LANDSCAPES

Depending on the kind of ecological interactions prevailing among a set or urban settings, different interaction landscapes can be constructed. In Section D.1 a two-urban settings interconnectance will be analysed and its *geographical* landscape will be drawn. In Section D.2 the urban Volterra–Lotka model of relative growth will be discussed, and its *economic* landscape will be shown.

1. A landscape of various urban geographies

Attention now turns to the geographic landscape of the general urban Volterra–Lotka model, and the stability properties of its various locales. Instead of considering the interaction of one city within a nation, an alternative perspective of the urban Volterra–Lotka model is taken. Assume two metropolitan areas, i and j, which *near their equilibrium points* (in the x_i, x_j space) affect each other in any of the three possible ways, shown in Table II.1.

TABLE II.1. *Combination of two-city interactions.* (They are captured in the scheme below.)

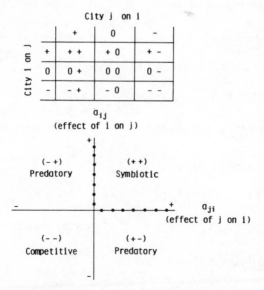

where along the dotted axes one $a > 0$ and the other is zero (commensal); along the other part of the axes one $a < 0$ and the other is zero (amensal); at the origin both a's are zero (isolative).

According to this Table, $(+ +)$ implies that both cities have positive effects upon each other's population size: in general ecology such connection is referred to as *symbiotic*; $(+ 0)$ implies that one city has a positive effect upon the other, without being affected by it in turn: this is a *commensal* relationship; $(+ -)$ implies that one city preys on the other, and this is the well-known *predatory* relationship among settings; $(- 0)$ implies *amensal* connection between two cities, so that one has a negative effect upon the other, without being in turn affected by it; $(- -)$ is a purely *competitive* relationship among two cities, so that each is antagonistic towards the other; and $(0\ 0)$ implies *isolation* between two cities. In summary, the six possible *urban geographies* for each pair of cities is as follows, where $a_1, a_{11}, a_2, a_{22} \gtrless 0; a_{12}, a_{21} > 0$

Symbiotic geography $(+ +)$

$$\dot{x}_1 = x_1(a_1 + a_{11}x_1 + a_{12}x_2)$$
$$\dot{x}_2 = x_2(a_2 + a_{21}x_1 + a_{22}x_2)$$

Commensal geography $(+ 0)$ or $(0 +)$

$$\dot{x}_1 = x_1(a_1 + a_{11}x_1 + a_{12}x_2) \qquad \dot{x}_1 = x_1(a_1 + a_{11}x_1)$$
$$\text{or:}$$
$$\dot{x}_2 = x_2(a_2 + a_{22}x_2) \qquad \dot{x}_2 = x_2(a_2 + a_{21}x_1 + a_{22}x_2)$$

Predatory geography $(+ -)$ or $(- +)$

$$\dot{x}_1 = x_1(a_1 + a_{11}x_1 + a_{12}x_2) \qquad \dot{x}_1 = x_1(a_1 + a_{11}x_1 - a_{12}x_2)$$
$$\text{or:}$$
$$\dot{x}_2 = x_2(a_2 - a_{21}x_1 + a_{22}x_2) \qquad \dot{x}_2 = x_2(a_2 + a_{21}x_1 + a_{22}x_2)$$

Amensal geography $(- 0)$ or $(0 -)$

$$\dot{x}_1 = x_1(a_1 + a_{11}x_1 - a_{12}x_2) \qquad \dot{x}_1 = x_1(a_1 + a_{11}x_1)$$
$$\text{or:}$$
$$\dot{x}_2 = x_2(a_2 + a_{22}x_2) \qquad \dot{x}_2 = x_2(a_2 - a_{21}x_1 + a_{22}x_2)$$

Competitive geography $(- -)$

$$\dot{x}_1 = x_1(a_1 + a_{11}x_1 - a_{12}x_2)$$
$$\dot{x}_2 = x_2(a_2 - a_{21}x_1 + a_{22}x_2)$$

Isolative geography (0 0)

$$\dot{x}_1 = x_1(a_1 + a_{11}x_1)$$

$$\dot{x}_2 = x_2(a_2 + a_{22}x_2)$$

One can construct an urban topological landscape as a result of the above analysis by considering the space of parameters a in the general system

$$\dot{x}_i = x_i(a_i + a_{ii}x_i + a_{ij}x_j)$$

$$\dot{x}_j = x_j(a_j + a_{jj}x_j + a_{ji}x_i)$$

with each parameter varying from $-\infty$ to $+\infty$, so that each point in the topological urban geographical space corresponds to a particular pair of urban areas at a particular time-period. There are points (in the neighbourhoods of zero parameter values as well as elsewhere) where bifurcation occurs in the geography type describing the urban ecosystem. If the parameters vary continuously for any pair of cities, due to technological innovation, changes in comparative advantages, or any other factor, one can trace a dynamic path on the topological space of successive geographies among the two cities.

It must be noted that there are two kinds of elements which contribute to the two-city dynamics discussed earlier. One is the direct effect of inter- or intra-city interaction manifested by the positivity (or negativity) of the a_{12}, a_{21}, and a_{11}, a_{22} coefficients. The other is due to all other factors affecting each city within a pertinent environment; it is represented by the magnitude of a_1 and a_2. These effects are separable under the Volterra–Lotka formalism.

One of the six schemes is familiar to urban geographers: the hierarchical structure of the central place theory is embedded in commensal-type connections. The upper level town is affected by the lower level, whereas the lower level is not affected by the size of the upper level city. The rest of the geographies have not attracted much attention in regional analysis, with the possible exception of Simmons (1982).

These six geographies do not appear to have quite equal chances of being observed. Three (commensal, amensal, and predatory) appear in the table of two-city interactions twice, whereas the other three (symbiotic, competitive, and isolative) appear once. Although, by itself, this is not a strong argument for supposing higher probability of occurrence, the stability properties of the six systems shed some light as to the likelihood of their being observed. Williamson (1972) and Slobodkin

(1961) have examined the stability of such interactions in general ecology. It seems that from all six geographies the commensal, amensal, and predatory are stable, whereas symbiotic and competitive are unstable May (1973). These results are obtained directly by applying the stability analysis discussed earlier to each type-model. This is of particular interest to urban geographical ecology as it relates to the local and global stability of the urban ecosystem. As some of the six geographies are not (locally in the landscape) stable, and given that most cities seem stable over extended time-periods, it is concluded that clusters of cities may lie on particular locations on the geographical landscape with a topography characterized by dynamic stability; the clusters must lie in valleys of negative real part eigenvalues.

Public policy must recognize the existence of such interactions and their critical points not only in policies of global urban intervention, but also in local actions. Policies aiming at slightly perturbing stable dynamic paths are bound to prove ineffective, since the geography-type of cities is not likely to change dramatically, unless the city is close to a singularity. It seems also that it is hardly desirable to promote policies aimed at enhancing either symbiotic or purely competitive modes of behaviour among cities either at the regional or national levels. The ultimate result of such policy actions promoting notions of symbiotic or purely competitive modes of urban connectance may have significant destabilizing effects upon the urban web of a nation or region, with the ultimate effect that one or more urban areas could be driven to extinction. More on policies will be added later.

Although the connections' sign in Table II.1 does not depend on the population levels for each pair of cities, this might not be a very restrictive assumption. If, however, the signs were to depend on specific levels of x_1, and/or x_2 then a much more complicated geography could emerge. When the connectance is not unimodal, but instead is a nonlinear function of x_1 and/or x_2 then there could be sets within the a-space belonging to a particular geography such that it would contain thresholds which when exceeded would abruptly shift the nature of the dynamic equilibria without changing the particular geography. These transitions would belong to the family of manifolds classified by catastrophe theory. Depending upon the degree of the polynomials involved near the equilibrium a particular catastrophe type in canonical form would describe the transitions.

In the urban geographical landscape (when these geographies are assumed to be drawn from a random distribution for any pair of cities), the probability of obtaining the particular ones which are of the amensal or commensal type (where the a_{12} or a_{21} are exactly zero) is vanishingly small. Thus the dominant geography with dynamical stability properties is the predatory one. It is not surprising then that this is the geography widely detected in one-city–nation interactions on relative population and factor reward for the US, by empirical studies (see Part II.E).

If reward equations are introduced in the two-city interaction, so that four simultaneous differential equations describe the two-city interconnection, then similar final connectance types can be drawn. However, the signs of these interactions will not depend on population interactions directly, but indirectly through the intermediate expected reward effects. This should not cause undue discomfort, however, since it only slightly changes the basic analysis.

2. The urban Volterra–Lotka model and urban economic landscapes

The analysis now returns to the particular urban Volterra–Lotka model of two differential equations depicting the interdependency between relative urban population and average factor reward for each metropolitan area, defined as

$$\dot{x} = x(a_1 + a_{11}x + a_{12}y)$$
$$\dot{y} = y(a_2 + a_{21}x + a_{22}y).$$

In a manner similar to the one outlining the existence of a variety of urban geographies when population levels between two towns interact, one can derive a variety of different *urban economies* when population and factor reward interact for a single city within a national environment. The reader is referred back to the previous Section which describes the variety of urban geographies, for a list of urban economic landscapes. There is no need for changing the basic terminology.

As a result of initial work by Dendrinos (1979), the following specification of the above model has been shown to be a good descriptor of relative urban growth, Dendrinos and Mullally (1982a, 1982b), where all parameters are positive

$$\dot{x} = x(a_1 - a_{11}x + a_{12}y)$$
$$\dot{y} = y(a_2 - a_{21}x).$$

The urban ecological model contains a subset of all possible economies embedded in the original Volterra–Lotka model, which in turn contains a subset of all possible economies when the general two-species version of the model is considered. None the less, the urban ecological model does contain a significant part of this general landscape of economies; they are the ones found in the vicinity of $a_{22} = 0$, as extensive simulation analysis indicates that for most of the US metropolitan areas there are no relative income scale effects. The particular cross-effects of this model are classified in the general ecological literature as predatory-type interactions, and thus the above specification is of the Volterra-Lotka predator–prey type.

A particular version of this model and the one used in this book, which allows for an interpretation of the various parameters and terms, is

$$\dot{x} = \alpha(y - \bar{y})x - \beta x^2$$
$$\dot{y} = \gamma(\bar{x} - x)y$$

where x denotes relative population size (normalized over a current national or regional total), and y is real (deflated) per capita income. Parameter $\bar{y}$ is the nationally (or regionally) prevailing deflated per capita income level, and $\bar{x}$ is the city's relative carrying capacity defined by its location in the national space. Per capita income corresponds to a level of total utility U_i gained in town i and equal to the prevailing national average $\bar{U}$. U_i is the sum of three components: a 'local' utility U_i^1 attained by consuming the equilibrium bundle of local commodities given the income earned; a 'size' effect, depicting a disutility U_i^2 due to negative externalities of population agglomeration; and a 'comparative' component U_i^3 associated with a ranking of desirability in locating at town i instead of any other place in the nation. U_i^3 could be due to positive effects of population concentration, or to the presence of amenities particular to that locale. Thus, $U_i = U_i^1 + U_i^2 + U_i^3 = \bar{U}$.

Parenthetically one might note that various components of a total utility function U may vary over time and space. Hardly would one expect the arguments of the utility function of a current US resident to be the same as two centuries ago, or that of a resident of Nepal. Some evolution in the utility function's form, or even in the entities entering the budget constraint, or in the type of relevant constraints must be expected.

In absence of U^2 and U^3 and given the connection between income and utility, one would expect income differentials to vanish when utility differentials vanish. All cities would settle at identical income and utility (U^1) levels equal to the national average $\bar{U}$. However, due to the existence of either heterogeneity in the national space and/or differential external effects of population concentrations, one does not observe such uniformity. Income differentials are not enough to pick up the changes in relative population size of cities. In the above specified urban Volterra–Lotka model, the net relative population change consists of an attraction and repulsion component. The term $\beta x^2/\alpha$ stands for the relative size and location related factors producing negative external effects of population agglomeration. It imposes a limit to growth due to relative congestion (friction), and it identifies the repulsive force. The term $(y - \bar{y})x$ is the attractive force; it includes relative size x, implying a preference for larger cities, and $y - \bar{y}$ depicting the pure effect of real per capita income differentials upon relative population accumulation. As long as $y > \bar{y}$ this factor is an attractive force but not enough by itself to attract additional population. When it drops below the national average it, too, becomes repulsive. In actuality, the national average $(\bar{y})$ is not the appropriate income level to derive driving income differentials, $y - \bar{y}$. Instead, there is a local income level $\bar{y}_i$ which must be used to compute the driving force. This income level $\bar{y}_i$ is an *expectation* among the nation's producers and consumers, which accounts for locational preferences associated with the attributes of U_3. In the US, however, it is found that $\bar{y}_i$'s do not vary significantly among the nation's SMSAs. Thus, in a first approximation and in order not to increase the number of parameters used in the urban Volterra–Lotka model, it is assumed that $\bar{y}_i$ are identical for all metropolitan areas and equal to the national average. Extensions involving different $\bar{y}_i$'s can accommodate, further, possible differences among producers' and consumers' expectations, as well as dynamic changes in these expectations. Parameter α is the speed for relative population accumulation (response per unit time). The end-result is a relative pull-minus-push factor in the x equation. As long as the pull factor exceeds the push, the relative city size will increase.

In the demand for relative population equation $(\dot{x})$, the motion ceases $(\dot{x} = 0)$ when y^* equals $\bar{y} + x^*\beta/\alpha$. Not all cities are expected to settle at identical income levels. The difference between any two cities' y^* identifies the total utility-constant per capita income equivalent differential. A higher steady-state per capita income level must identify the necessary income requirement for compensating the disutility due to negative external effects of agglomeration. On the supply side $(\dot{y})$, motion ceases when the city's relative carrying capacity has been reached. Income generating opportunities will be extracted from the city's stock up to $\bar{x}$, when other localities will start becoming attractive. Variable $\bar{x}$ can also be interpreted as an expectation from the nation's producers and consumers. Parameter γ is the relative speed in per capita income accumulation. The clockwise oscillatory motion of the above system is shown in the phase portrait of Fig. II.4(b).

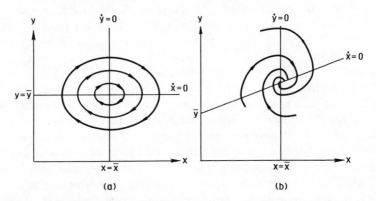

FIG. II.4. *The two variables Volterra–Lotka dynamics*
(a) neutrally stable orbits when $\beta = 0$ (centre-type dynamic equilibrium);
(b) sink spiralling behaviour when $y = \bar{y} + \beta/\alpha \, x$.

From a stability standpoint the above model produces sink spiral type equilibria, indicating oscillatory convergence to a stable steady state. Thus the single-city urban ecological model with a reward function produces stability. The stability conditions are global in the x, y space since a Liapunof function can be constructed for the above model. Kolmogoroff (1936) has shown the possibility for existence of stable (on both sides) limit cycles in a two-species general Volterra–Lotka system. A more recent paper on the subject is that by Brauer (1979). The conditions imposed upon the f and g functions for such a phenomenon to occur, are that in the general system

$$\frac{dx}{dt} = x \, f(x,y)$$

$$\frac{dy}{dt} = y \, g(x,y)$$

$$\frac{\partial f}{\partial y} > 0; \quad \frac{df}{d\left(\dfrac{x}{y}\right)} > 0; \quad f(0,0) < 0.$$

Further, there exists large numbers $L, M > 0$ such that $f(0, L) = 0$ and $f(M, 0) = 0$. With regard to the g function:

$$\frac{\partial g}{\partial y} > 0; \quad \frac{dg}{d\left(\frac{x}{y}\right)} > 0;$$

and there exists $N > 0$ such that $g(N, 0) = 0$. Also, $N < M$. All of the above conditions are applicable with the urban Volterra–Lotka system with the exception of $\partial g/\partial y > 0$. This condition requires that we introduce income agglomeration effects, an element which does not affect the analysis at all. Thus, the previous urban Volterra–Lotka system extended appropriately could admit limit cycles when urban areas can be found which satisfy the slightly modified Kolmogoroff conditions for a stable limit cycle. Under the income agglomeration effects formulation the urban Volterra–Lotka system can exhibit the Hopf bifurcation which transforms sinks to stable limit cycles through a centre. Parenthetically, when the coefficients of the original system are such that

$$a_{11} = a_{22} = 0; \; a_{12}a_{21} < 0; \; a_1a_2 < 0$$

then the system becomes a conservative Volterra–Lotka model with harmonic motion. This is a neutrally stable motion with increasing amplitude further from the centre and with approximate period $T = \dfrac{2\pi}{a_1a_2}$.

Structural stability analysis of the above system as the coefficient β varies (presumably due to alteration of internal circumstances as a result of investment in alleviating urban congestion or other externalities of agglomeration) produces a simple bifurcation at the vicinity of $\beta = 0$ when the sink is transformed into a centre associated with orbital motion in the phase portrait. This is so because the real part becomes zero and only the imaginary part of the eigenvalues remains. Since the probability that $\beta = 0$ at any particular time-period at any city is vanishingly small, the chance of observing periodic motion in urban dynamics must be very small. Empirical evidence seems to support this conclusion. No regular periodic motion over the time-period surveyed was detected, with one possible exception (the Rochester SMSA). This observation must also exclude the premise of stable limit cycles (i.e. more complex dynamic models).

E. EMPIRICAL FINDINGS: URBAN EVOLUTIONARY PATTERNS

In this section the general results from testing efforts towards vali-
dating empirically the urban Volterra–Lotka relative growth model are
presented. An overview and summary of the numerical simulations,
covering the period 1940–77 and at certain instances the 1890–1980
time-span, for a number of US metropolitan areas are given in section
E.1. The subject of perturbations due to environmental changes is
addressed in section E.2, where the proper and apparent motion in dynamical trajectories are defined. In section E.3 the urban perturbations
are presented as recorded for two US SMSAs. The material in these two
sections is related to the parameter shifting phenomenon.

Following these, section E.4 addresses the issue of urban carrying
capacities as obtained through the computer simulations, together with
the notion of 'effective environments'. In section E.5 the topic of urban
clocks, i.e. the period of motion in aggregate relative urban dynamics
is discussed. A few associations between these variables and other key
characteristics of metropolitan areas (size, age, location, etc.) are
provided.

1. Overview

A brief review of the testing efforts is presented at first. Most of the
findings have been reported in the literature earlier, although some new
findings are added. The results cover mostly the period 1940–77 and
they are based solely on relative population dynamics. More recent
testing covering the period 1890–1980, with the inclusion of actual
data on relative per capita income for the period 1959-80, is also
reported here.

In an effort to validate the urban ecological theory and extract topics
of special importance to the urban context, and thus appropriately
extend the general ecological framework, a survey of metropolitan
areas of one nation was carried out. The survey covered the universe of
the Standard Metropolitan Statistical Areas in the United States – 265
as of 1977. It included the records of the dynamic paths of their relative
metropolitan population and their individually deflated (whenever
possible) per capita income ratio over the US average counts for the
period 1940–77. Detailed results of the survey have been reported elsewhere (Dendrinos and Mullally, 1982a, 1982b). Here a synthesis and
certain extensions are supplied in view of some new findings. Numerical
computer simulation of twenty-eight US SMSAs was conducted using

the Runge–Kutta method of estimating solutions to systems of differential equations. The subroutine DVERK of the International Mathematical and Statistical Library (IMSL) was used to simulate the urban Volterra–Lotka model

$$\dot{x} = \alpha(y - 1)x - \beta x^2$$
$$\dot{y} = \gamma(\bar{x} - x)y$$

where x here is the relative population size of a metropolitan area normalized over the total US population at time-period t, and y is the ratio of the urban real per capita income to the prevailing national average during each time-period t. The results are shown in Table II.2.

Few notes regarding these simulations. Due to lack of comparable time-series data on per capita income and their deflators over the entire time-period (1940–77), in earlier studies only relative population size was calibrated for. This restriction has been relaxed in later studies where income is incorporated, and shown for one particular SMSA (Minneapolis–St Paul on Table II.4), and the time-period has been extended from 1890 to 1980.

No formal statistical tests have been carried out. Such tests and needed confirmation is waiting further data collection and studies by other researchers. However, for a strategic-type model such as this, one can draw satisfaction in seeing that the essential qualitative features of the model replicate empirical evidence at a satisfactory level.

Looking at the simulated dynamic paths of US metropolitan areas it is concluded that the most commonly exhibited dynamic, which can replicate observed relative population movements over time, obeys spiralling sink type behaviour (Fig. II.4 (b)). The major qualitative feature of the model, in one state variable, is that larger amplitude oscillations be followed by lower amplitude ones over time. For those SMSAs with a period less than the observation period this phenomenon seems to be generally valid. Examples include the Tacoma, Toledo, and Terre-Haute SMSAs discussed in Dendrinos and Mullally (1982a).

Thus, aggregate urban dynamic behaviour, normalized within a national environment, exhibits stability. The urban sector of the US, at least, is dynamically stable over the time-period that recorded evidence allows for study. Neither spiralling nor node type sources, or saddles can replicate observed dynamic paths of relative urban size consistently for all SMSAs. This finding is of interest because, unless contradicted by future empirical evidence, it seems to support the main claim that

TABLE II.2.   *Parameters*[1] *of the Volterra–Lotka model for 17 US metropolitan areas for 1940–77; and 11 for 1890–1980 (indicated by* †*)*

SMSA[2]	α	β	γ	Period[3]	$\bar{x}$[4]	y^*[5]
Atlanta	1.080	.0185	.0015	34	8.90	1.163
Birmingham (AL)	1.344	.0215	.0022	35	3.85	1.068
Chicago†	.312	.0180	.0002	120	23.00	1.137
Denver†	.562	.0117	.0010	135	8.00	1.143
Detroit†	.336	.0026	.0009	80	20.60	1.184
Houston†	.452	.0071	.0008	140	14.00	1.250
Kansas City	1.344	.0196	.0024	25	6.07	1.099
Los Angeles†	.605	.0064	.0013	90	32.50	1.766
Miami	1.456	.0174	.0009	40	5.90	1.078
Minneapolis†	.896	.0143	.0018	90	9.25	1.163
New Haven	2.912	.0465	.0052	14	3.62	1.063
New Orleans	1.140	.0175	.0022	30	4.34	1.090
New York†	1.120	.0130	.0020	160	38.00	1.350
Philadelphia†	.254	.0158	.0020	250	12.00	1.214
Phoenix	.560	.0141	.0010	80	4.55	1.128
Pittsburgh†	2.300	.0124	.0002	90	7.00	1.125
Rochester	1.792	.0000	.0040	17	4.40	1.000
San Francisco†	.344	.0149	.0015	70	14.00	1.250
Seattle	1.568	.0225	.0024	23	6.60	1.106
St Cloud	2.800	.0448	.0050	17	.69	1.011
St Louis†	.313	.0501	.0056	180	8.00	1.143
Tacoma	2.240	.0590	.0060	11	1.96	1.057
Terre-Haute	4.472	.0716	.0104	17	.82	1.014
Toledo	3.357	.0483	.0051	13	3.65	1.058
Tucson	.896	.0193	.0012	45	1.20	1.033
Tulsa	4.480	.0716	.0080	12	2.61	1.046
Wichita	7.168	.0934	.0128	8	1.93	1.029
York	6.272	.1002	.0112	10	1.62	1.029

[1] The parameters are in yearly intervals
[2] Only the first central city is identified
[3] Elapsed calendar time between a local max and min in normalized population size (NPS), (or relative factor reward)
[4] Steady-state (NPS in 10^3), i.e. carrying capacity
[5] Steady-state income ratio to the US average
Source: Dendrinos and Mullally (1982b), for the 1940–77 cases

a simple dynamic system can be used to simulate a seemingly very complicated process, namely relative urban growth. This system is a simple predator-prey type model.

This in turn has ramifications upon the investigator's design search for an appropriate dynamic model. It is rather easy, in dynamical analysis, to construct difference or differential equations systems that would do almost anything, including multiple dynamic equilibria. The evidence suggests that such systems may be needlessly complicated for the purpose at hand.

A typical SMSA which exhibits simulated damped oscillatory motion is the Denver-Boulder metropolitan area (Fig. II.5). In part (a) of the figure the numerically derived path is shown, projected into the future, together with Denver-Boulder's steady state. In Fig. II.5 (b) the simulated and actual counts for relative population are given. The case of the Milwaukee SMSA is shown in Table II.3 with the parameter values used to simulate the 1890-1980 dynamic path of the Milwaukee normalized population size. Milwaukee is another typical US metropolitan area exhibiting spiralling sink behaviour.

The urban system of the US seems to be dynamically stable, when viewed through the relative population-income lens, because it consists of individually dissipative urban systems. All cities surveyed are characterized by positive β (i.e. presence of relative friction), and absence of either positive or negative income agglomeration effects. Evidence is found, reported in Dendrinos (1983), that one urban area, the Rochester, New York SMSA, exhibits in the 1940-77 period a

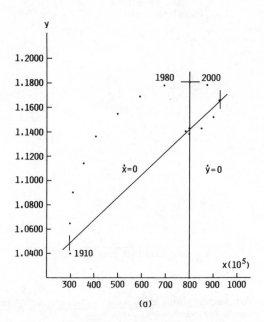

FIG. II.5. *The Denver-Boulder metropolitan area.* (a) *Simulated counts for relative population size* (x) *and per capita income ratio* (y).

dynamic path which seems to be close to an orbital motion (observed when $\beta = 0$), Fig. II.4 (a). Rochester is the only candidate found so far to suggest the presence of possible bifurcation in US relative metropolitan dynamics. Whether it implies that in metropolitan aggregate dynamics a negative Hopf bifurcation is present (negative because a stable limit cycle is transformed into a focus, instead of a focus being transformed into a stable limit cycle); or that a simple sink is transformed to neutrally stable orbits is a matter of further empirical analysis.

The selected sample of cities from the US urban sector consistently required a positive parameter β. One must dismiss a possible 'local' character in the x, y space, since the urban ecological model, being of the predator-prey variety, does exhibit global stability conditions in the x, y space. One can easily derive a Liapunof function for it, see Hirsch

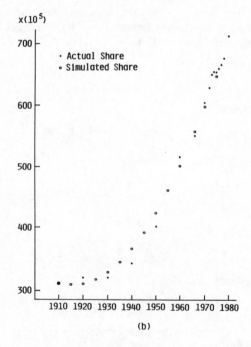

FIG. II.5. *The Denver–Boulder metropolitan area.* (b) *Actual and simulated counts for relative population.*
Actual share.
Simulated share.

TABLE II.3. *The 1890–1980 Milwaukee, Wisconsin SMSA dynamic path*

Year	Population size (sim) 10^5	Population size[1] (act) 10^5	Factor reward (sim)	Simulation parameters
1890	487.0	486.8	1.0600	$x_0 = 487.0$
1900	514.5	530.8	1.0680	$y_0 = 1.06$
1910	549.4	553.7	1.0735	$\bar{x} = 600.00$
1920	588.0	587.9	1.0760	$y^* = 1.055$
1930	625.0	666.7	1.0755	$\alpha = 1.12$
1940	654.9	661.4	1.0722	$\beta = .01$
1950	674.2	665.9	1.0669	$\gamma = .003$
1960	680.1	707.9	1.0607	period: 90 years
1966	678.2	679.2	1.0569	
1967	677.3	675.8	1.0503	
1970	674.6	684.7	1.0544	
1971	673.3	683.8	1.0539	
1972	672.0	680.8	1.0533	
1973	670.8	671.0	1.0528	
1974	664.5	666.8	1.0522	
1975	667.9	653.3	1.0517	
1976	666.4	650.8	1.0512	
1977	664.8	643.4	1.0506	
1978	663.2	636.6	1.0501	
1980	659.6	613.6	1.0492	

Source: [1] US Department of Commerce, Bureau of the Census, P-25 Reports, various years

and Smale (1974). Thus the model is capable of depicting metropolitan behaviour close as well as far from equilibrium. A negative β would mean that the $\dot{x} = 0$ isocline ($y = \bar{y} + \beta/\alpha x$) would have a negative slope, intersecting (if at all) the $\dot{y} = 0$ isocline ($x = \bar{x}$) at levels below the national average. An intersection of any of the isoclines in the negative part of the x, y axis could imply extinction. This type of intersection has not been encountered in the metropolitan areas surveyed. Thus selection processes in the urban sector of nations must favour stability. Much more will be said on this issue in Part IV.

Another major conclusion derived from the US case of single-city urban ecologies operating within a national environment is that all SMSAs in reference to the US occupy collectively in the urban economic landscape a very limited area in the space of $\alpha > 0, \beta \geqslant 0, \gamma > 0$. Further, the three parameters which define the dimensions of the urban economic landscape vary within a rather narrow window in the positive part of their axis. Inter-urban variability seems to be indeed very limited. The aggregate urban code, although capable of containing a vast variety of performance, exhibits a schedule with surprisingly limited variety in reproduction. These topics are further elaborated in Part IV.

Examining the values of the parameters α and γ it is found that the former is 100 times greater than the latter. This may imply that there is a relatively fast dynamic present at the population adjustment process and a relatively slow one at the income adjustment process. This presents certain interesting extensions of the model along the lines of catastrophe theory, if higher-order terms are introduced into the population adjustment equation. One could derive a manifold associated with the relative population accumulation process comprised of fast equilibria (Zeeman, 1972), on either surface of which paths are traced derived from the relative income accumulation dynamic

$$e\dot{x} = x\Big(\alpha(y - 1) - \beta x\Big)$$
$$\dot{y} = \gamma y(\bar{x} - x).$$

Parameter e depicts a fast foliation upon the surface of a fold-type catastrophe. If the congestion term is cubic, βx^3, then the fast foliation is toward a cusp's surface where the income accumulation equation represents a slow movement. Extensions along the Van der Pol equation are also possible here, if empirical evidence is presented which demonstrates more involved dynamic phenomena. It is also found that parameter α varies proportionally less than γ. This can be attributed to higher variability (and propensity to move) at the supply side among different locales, than variability to utility of residence.

So far testing has focused upon the observed relative population size. This variable is much more reliable than relative per capita income; it is also available over longer time-periods due to availability of data from decennial census reports on county population counts. Counts on per capita income are rather recent. The result is that evidence regarding the relative per capita income performance of the models must be approached with caution. A reminder here is that this count is only a proxy for a more inclusive relative factor reward. Lack of per capita income counts from census of population sources is compensated by comparable counts from the *Survey of Current Business* for those SMSAs whose county composition has not been altered for the period 1959–80. The Minneapolis–St Paul SMSA is presented (Table II.4) with the actual and simulated counts for the corresponding years on relative

TABLE II.4. *The Minneapolis–St. Paul SMSA numerical simulation:*
1890–1980

Year	Population size		Income ratio		Simulated parameters
	(sim) 10^5	(act)[1] 10^5	(sim)	(act)[2]	
1890	744.00	743.6	1.0600		$x_O = 744.0$
1900	711.35	736.5	1.0746		$y_O = 1.06$
1910	719.99	781.3	1.0901		$\bar{x} = 925.0$
1920	760.39	781.1	1.1040		$y^* = 1.104$
1930	821.29	791.6	1.1143		$\alpha = .633$
1940	889.22	804.0	1.1198		$\beta = .007$
1950	949.06	822.2	1.1205		$\gamma = .0012$
1959	986.02		1.1178	1.1665	period: 70 years
1960	988.84	884.5	1.1174		
1965	999.71		1.1151	1.1526	
1966	1001.17	890.3	1.1145		
1969	1004.10		1.1130	1.1629	
1970	1004.74	958.3	1.1124		
1971	1005.00	957.3	1.1119		
1972	1005.19	948.1	1.1113	1.1083	
1973	1005.09	944.7	1.1108	1.1085	
1974	1004.87	944.6	1.1102	1.1107	
1975	1004.45	935.8	1.1097	1.1183	
1976	1003.85	933.3	1.1091	1.1192	
1977	1003.12	928.5	1.1086	1.1256	
1978	1002.19	926.8	1.1080	1.1036	
1979	1001.18		1.1075	1.1573	
1980	999.95	928.6	1.1070	1.1863	

Sources: [1] US Department of Commerce, Bureau of the Census, P-25 Reports,
various years; [2] US Department of Commerce, Bureau of the Census,
Survey of Current Business, various years.

population size and real (deflated) per capita income ratio. A per capita
income deflator for Minneapolis–St Paul and one for the US have been
used.

Parameter values (not in yearly intervals) responsible for this computer simulation are: $\alpha = .633$, $\beta = .007$, $\gamma = .0012$. The simulation
provides strong support for the urban ecological model. The average
deviation in the income count is about 3.5 per cent whereas in the
population count is about 6.4 per cent. More importantly, the qualitative patterns of the relative population size and per capita income
ratio are replicated by the simulated patterns: a high reached in per
capita income count in the 1950s is picked up in the simulation runs,
together with a low in relative population size in the 1910s, and a high

in relative population size at the beginning of the 1970s. During the 1970s, Minneapolis–St Paul is close to its steady state, found through numerical simulations to be around $x^* = 925.0 \times 10^{-5}$ and $y^* = 1.104$. The main qualitative feature of the predator–prey model is that, at particular parts in the phase portrait, while one variable increases, the other declines. This feature is depicted in the Minneapolis–St Paul case: as the population share was increased in the 1950–70 period, the per capita income ratio declined. Since about 1970 the relative size of Minneapolis–St Paul is continuously declining accompanied by declines in the per capita income ratio. The latter feature cannot be captured by the urban economic model of Fig. II.1.

2. *Apparent and proper motion in aggregate urban dynamics*

This section deals with issues of shifts in parameter values due to shocks. It is argued that such shifts are not frequent in relative metropolitan dynamics, and when they occur seemingly obey certain regularities, indicating that their effects are not random. A metropolitan area's motion in the relative population–income space is the combination of two movements: the movement toward a steady state, predominantly a spiralling sink; and the motion due to a shift in the steady state. The first will be referred to as the 'proper' motion and the combined movement as a result of the shift in the equilibrium point will be referred to as the 'apparent' motion. The proper motion is endogenous to a city; as it will be seen in Part IV it is a mechanism of adjustment to a static environment, whereas, the apparent motion is due to environmental changes. The apparent motion is associated with a slow equilibrium: the proper motion is attached to a fast equilibrium. If the recorded dynamic paths of the US SMSAs are shown to be mostly due to shifts of the attractor, then the conclusions drawn earlier may be questioned. Thus, acceptance of these conclusions critically hinges upon the assumption that the behaviour of the steady state in the time-span examined is mostly static. It is noted that over short time-periods one might be induced into seeing more frequently 'apparent' motions, than in longer time-spans, where perturbations smooth out and the mean trajectory is a 'proper' motion.

　　If one were to accept that the steady state of the metropolitan areas in the US were to move frequently (in the thirty-seven-year time-horizon of the study period for seventeen SMSAs and the ninety-year time-period for the remaining eleven) one ought to expect a random motion in a sample of SMSAs. Changes in the equilibrium population and income levels of SMSAs are due to shocks (endogenous and/or exogenous) of an urban setting: they comprise technological innovations, shifts in preferences, changes in availability of input factors in production and prices, shifts in output markets, etc. Such *ad hoc* perturbations must be randomly distributed over time, varied in magnitude, and must affect differently the various urban settings. Consequently, if these events were frequent enough to be captured within the observation period, they ought to have produced a seemingly random motion in the behaviour of SMSAs in the population–income space.

But the observed paths were not classified as random, instead they were shown to exhibit qualitative properties consistent with dynamic models of the Volterra–Lotka type. In the rare case where perturbations did occur, computer simulation was capable of reproducing precisely the underlying changes in model parameters, and a certain consistency was found in these changes as shown in Section E.3. No random motion was detected.

Either of the following two conclusions can be drawn. One is that random events are not very frequent and thus not recorded in the ninety-year span. This is rather unacceptable in view of the evidence: a number of significant nation-wide shocks did take place, and the urban areas of the US have witnessed ample technological and behavioural changes during these years. The widespread use of the automobile, changes in production and consumption conditions, as well as in the functions of government, various economic and demographic changes, suburbanization of the employment and residential activities are among the most notable. We are left with the alternative conclusion: such shocks affect only selectively the steady state of cities which in their vast majority exhibit a resiliency towards these shocks. This proposition admits that the relative position, in terms of comparative advantages, a city occupies within a nation does not change frequently (that is, within approximately a 100-year time-period).

The following appears to be a representative history of aggregate inter-urban dynamics: SMSAs spend most of their time on a motion toward their steady state in relative population and per capita income. In exhibiting this dynamic path they exhaust a potential for income (output) accumulation imposed upon them by the comparative advantages they enjoy within the national economy. As they come closer to filling that production capacity they become vulnerable to perturbations. These perturbations (which must not last long since not detected in ninety-year periods for selected SMSAs) shift the older SMSAs toward a new steady state. This new long-term equilibrium could be associated with lower/higher relative population and per capita income (Minneapolis–St Paul, p. 61). More evidence needs to be collected to be able to ascertain exactly what occurs when SMSAs approach close enough their long-run equilibrium. In Fig. II.6 the observed dynamic paths of three relatively old and large SMSAs are shown, together with their simulated trajectories.

From recent history we know that in older and larger SMSAs certain attempts have been made to partially refill the depleted income potential. Through the re-use of old and depreciated capital stock, or through small-scale new capital investment, coupled with a new composition of the labour force, it seems that the industrial base of these metropolitan areas is altered, from predominantly manufacturing to services. Although the whole US economy seems to be shifting along these lines, this change is particularly pronounced in the older and larger metropolitan areas. Whether these processes are of the drastic nature implied here, or mere short-term trends, remains to be seen.

3. Urban perturbations

Changes in the values of parameters defining the urban (geographic or economic) landscape need not be exclusively smooth, continuous, or infinitesimally small. As long as perturbations (or fluctuations, or oscillations) of these parameters do not carry them across boundaries delineating different geographies or economies these events are of a non-evolutionary nature: they shift a metropolitan area from one steady state to another similar state, or from one trajectory to a neighbouring one. It was mentioned earlier that shorter horizons are more likely to reveal discernible fluctuations. None was found in the ninety-year period.

By looking at a relative snapshot of metropolitan dynamics (the 1940–77 period), empirical evidence seems to uncover discontinuous, small and large, short- and long-lived perturbations that either died out or had some medium-term effect upon particular SMSAs. Two cases are of interest. The Miami SMSA experienced a perturbation which shifted the metropolitan area to a neighbouring path (Fig. II.7 (a)). This perturbation still leads Miami to its original steady state in the relative population–reward space, however, by a neighbouring path. In the case of the Seattle–Everett SMSA the effect was to shift the urban area to a different dynamic equilibrium altogether: from one steady state to a neighbouring one (Fig. II.7 (b)).

Timing of these perturbations is of interest. The Miami and Seattle–Everett events occurred in the mid-sixties and were short-lived, lasting

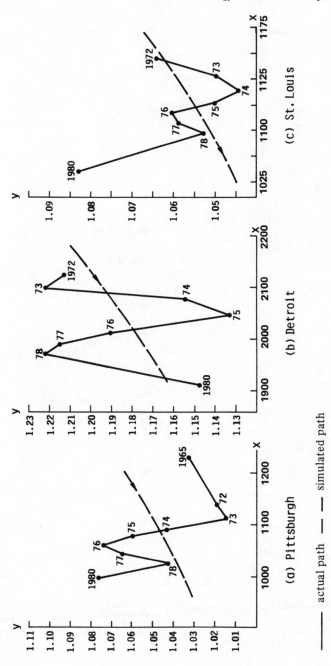

FIG. II.6. *Oscillations in the case of three large and old metropolitan areas: on their way to their steady state (1965–80)* Variable x is the relative population size (10^5); y is the relative per capita income (in constant terms — using SMSA and US deflators)

—— actual path — — simulated path

(a) Pittsburgh

(b) Detroit

(c) St. Louis

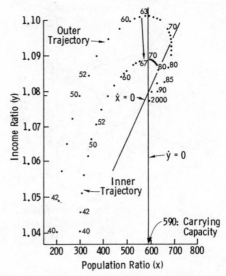

(a) The perturbation of Miami's spiral sink
    path from an outer to an inner one.

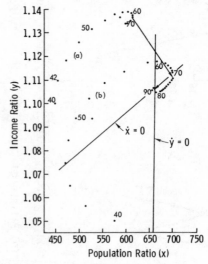

(b) Seattle's shift of trajectory from (a) to (b)

FIG. II.7.   *Perturbations of the dynamic equilibria for two metropolitan
areas. Source:* Dendrinos and Mullally (1983)

about six calendar years. Both resulted in a steady state with an expected lower relative reward level; in the case of Seattle the perturbation resulted in an expected rise in its steady-state relative population level (carrying capacity). Both metropolitan areas are middle-sized SMSAs and relatively young.

4. *The urban carrying capacity and the effective environment of cities*

A key feature of the urban ecological model is the existence of a relative carrying capacity characterizing all urban areas of a nation or region. The difference between the 'urban' carrying capacity and the term as used in ecology is noted. In general ecology carrying capacity having been reached implies local births equal local deaths. The carrying capacity in the urban ecological model outlined earlier is the steady-state relative population level. In the explicit relative dynamics of the model whenever a city's carrying capacity is exceeded the SMSA's relative per capita income declines. This is because other SMSAs not yet having reached their carrying capacities become more attractive.

The carrying capacity level of population is not a parameter determined endogenously by a particular city. Rather it depends upon the effective environment within which the open urban area operates. The simulation procedures involved in the Volterra–Lotka model allows for estimating each city's relative carrying capacity $\bar{x}$. As discussed earlier the robustness of this carrying capacity within the recorded time-span is quite considerable. This persistence indicates the metropolitan area's ties to its environment are sticky and thus rather stable over such time-horizons.

Most of the statements made earlier on the behaviour of US metropolitan areas were associated with normalizing each city's urban population and average per capita income to the US total population and per capita income correspondingly. These totals identify the environment within which an urban area unfolds its economic landscape which is identified by the type of Volterra–Lotka urban ecological system postulated. Now a closer look is taken as to the role of this environment in relative growth/decline patterns.

In a relative growth/decline framework x depicts the ratio of an urban area's population level X_i to the nation's population X; and y defines the ratio of the city's per capita income Y_i to the nation's per capita income Y. Thus, the kinetic equations expressed in X_i, X, Y_i and Y are

$$\dot{x} = (e-1) \, X_i \frac{\partial X}{\partial t} \Big/ X^2$$

$$e = \left(\frac{\partial X_i}{\partial t} \Big/ X_i\right) \Big/ \left(\frac{\partial X}{\partial t} \Big/ X\right)$$

$$\dot{y} = (h-1) \, Y_i \frac{\partial Y_i}{\partial t} \Big/ Y^2$$

$$h = \left(\frac{\partial Y_i}{\partial t} \Big/ Y_i\right) \Big/ \left(\frac{\partial Y}{\partial t} \Big/ Y\right)$$

where e and h represent the ratio of the city's growth-rates in population and income to these of the nation. In other words, e and h are the elasticities of urban growth with regard to the national growth; if e and h are greater than one, $\dot{x}$ and $\dot{y}$ are positive. Not all kinds of normalizations can produce meaningful dynamics. These particular ones with which one can attribute some theoretical understanding and empirical verification will be associated with 'effective environments'.

Change in the environment would imply a different normalization process. If a particular region is to be tested as an effective environment then that region's total population and per capita income are to be used as normalizing factors. Besides the normalized population and factor reward levels, the effects on a particular SMSA of different environments are reflected in its relative carrying capacity, friction coefficient, and speeds of adjustment. However, such shifts of environments mean different forms of the economic landscape associated with different dynamical systems. Not all possible environments can be described by Volterra–Lotka dynamics, or any other non-random dynamical behaviour for a given metropolitan area, or set of areas. Thus, not all conceivable environments are effective ones. Empirical evidence suggests that the US national economy *in toto* is an effective environment for all SMSAs studied. So is the US total urban sector (Dendrinos and Mullally, 1982b). Both give rise to urban economic landscapes capable of being adequately described by a Volterra–Lotka system on normalized population and per capita income counts. In a topological sense these two effective environments (the nation and its urban sector) are neighbouring environments of the metropolitan areas in the US, both producing qualitatively equivalent economic landscapes.

Although the two environments give qualitatively equivalent geographies and economies, the dynamic paths of a given urban area within these two landscapes, corresponding to the two environments, may be quite different. *The behaviour of an urban setting is not independent of the environment within which this setting is viewed.* This relativistic perspective had eluded conventional analysis. The misleading and erroneous conclusions one can draw from such omission can easily be seen in attempts to forecast absolute urban population levels based on past population trends. Cases in point include attempts to forecast population of primate cities in developing countries. These forecasts using simple linear projections of short-term trends in absolute population counts border on the absurd. Certain projections for Mexico City reaching 35 million people by the year 2000 are cases in point, see Ward (1981). In the proposed perspective a city must be viewed as an element in a hierarchical decomposition of a national economy from a higher more aggregate level to a lower one, as long as these levels create effective environments for a city in question.

The oscillatory urban motion and its associated periodicity obtains now a new perspective. Cities oscillate in their relative population-income space as a response to an equilibration process operating within a particular environment. As there might be a number of such environments there are an equal number of possible dynamic paths. Of interest are these particular environments which produce in qualitative terms distinctly different paths. A city's absolute motion is a topological transformation of all motions in all thus defined environments. Not all these motions must necessarily belong to the same type of urban economic or geographical landscape. The more environments a city's relative dynamic behaviour is traced in a non-random fashion and the more one knows about the dynamics of these environments, the more confident one is of the absolute dynamics of the particular city. However, the number of effective environments for a particular city may say a lot about the dynamic stability of the city's absolute population and factor reward.

Is there a bound to the number of effective environments for a given city? The answer is not immediately obvious. However, if the number of the effective environments for a group of cities were to be relatively large then a nation's (or region's) individual metropolitan areas could exhibit absolute dynamic patterns not characterized by any regularity. Over the recorded period the urban sector of the US, however, exhibits elements of such regularity. The conclusion must be drawn that the number of effective environments for a given set of urban areas must be small. This proposition ought to hold independently of the choice of sets of cities. Enlargements in the number of effective environments for a particular city must decrease the likelihood of regular absolute growth patterns. Effective environments change partly as inter-regional transportation costs decline through investment in transport and inter-regional accessibility increases. This can be of interest to spatial analysts.

5. *Period of motion and summary*

Since orbital (neutrally stable) motion is not to be found in abundance in metropolitan histories (possibly only one such case is detected in the case of the US — the Rochester SMSA — and this may be a short-lived event unless we are faced with a stable limit cycle) urban clocks strictly equivalent to the biological or physical ones do not exist. However, there is periodicity involved in a spiralling sink motion as the elapsed calendar time between a local minimum (in either population or income counts) and a local maximum remains constant for any given SMSA. In the population–income space, the damped oscillation covers less ground when close to equilibrium and more ground when further away from it. Thus, urban relative growth/decline cycles are much more pronounced when the urban area is further from its long-run equilibrium.

By looking at Table II.2, particular connection can be identified between period of motion in urban dynamics and size: the larger the size the longer the period. It seems that regional location within the nation, or age are not directly related to period lengths.

In summary: the relative population and per capita income aggregate dynamics of a single city in reference to the nation were shown to be described by a spiralling sink type dynamic equilibrium. Evidence for a Hopf bifurcation was presented in the case of the US urban sector. Relative carrying capacities exist for each city relative to the national economy. When approached, cities may exhibit violent outbursts: they shift toward a new steady state where, as a result, the urban carrying capacities are upwardly or downwardly adjusted. The nation was shown to be an effective environment, but multiple such environments may exist in urban dynamics. Finally, the period of the damped oscillatory motion in the urban Volterra–Lotka model was found to be directly related to steady-state city size.

F. MULTIPLE CITIES INTERACTION: URBAN COMPLEXITY AND STABILITY

The following part addresses the simultaneous *n*-population interaction urban model. It draws in Section F.1 from previous and basic work by

May on complexity vs. stability and builds the argument that inter-urban connectivity is highly selective and non-random. Earlier work in mathematical ecology by Volterra is also used to prove certain powerful theorems regarding absolute urban growth patterns (Section F.2). Some of these results are of interest in studying the urban sector of developing countries. Finally, the Section concludes with a model in which the May results are utilized in an economic general competitive equilibrium framework (Section F.3).

1. Urban ecosystems with random interaction: the May theorem

Assume that a number of cities I interact so that their *absolute* population and reward accumulation levels are given by

$$\dot{x}_i = x_i F_i^1 (x_1(t), \ldots x_I(t); y_1(t) \ldots y_I(t))$$

$$\dot{y}_i = y_i F_i^2 (x_1(t), \ldots x_I(t); y_1(t) \ldots y_I(t))$$

where the form of the functions F_i^1, F_i^2 depend upon the particular city i $(F_i^1 \neq F_i^2$ for the same i; and $F_i^1 \neq F_j^1$). Equilibrium away from the origin implies

$$F_i^1 (x_i^*, y_i^*; \quad i = 1, 2, \ldots, I) = 0$$

$$F_i^2 (x_i^*, y_i^*; \quad i = 1, 2, \ldots, I) = 0$$

for all i's in I. This is a set of $2I$ simultaneous, in general non-linear, equations on x_i^*'s and y_i^*'s. Following the standard stability analysis procedures, by linearly approximating around the equilibrium point(s) discarding higher-order terms of the corresponding Taylor series expansion, the qualitative properties of the system when subject to slight disturbances can be obtained.

If any of the linearized system's eigenvalues has a positive real part then the whole system is unstable. If one or more of these eigenvalues is/are pure imaginary then the system has neutral stability. Finally the system is stable if and only if all eigenvalues have negative real parts. Slight perturbations will grow, but the local stability analysis is unable to tell us what will occur globally. It is possible that as higher-order terms (either negative or positive externalities of agglomeration) become more important the metropolitan area(s) will either become extinct or grow beyond any bound of large urban agglomeration. Finally, they could encounter points of bifurcation associated with sudden change in direction of movement. Stronger conclusions can be drawn from a more specific formulation.

Assume the F functions of the previous urban ecological system to be linear, for both population and reward accumulations

$$\dot{x}_i = x_i(a_i^1 + \sum_{j=1}^{I} \alpha_{ij}x_j + \sum_{j=1}^{I} \beta_{ij}y_j) = H_i^1$$

$$\dot{y}_i = y_i(a_i^2 + \sum_{j=1}^{I} \gamma_{ij}x_j + \sum_{j=1}^{I} \delta_{ij}y_j) = H_i^2$$

and the requirement that the coefficients are such that positive values of x and y are obtained at the equilibrium point(s). At equilibrium slight disturbances produce

$$x_i = x_i^* (1 + \epsilon_i)$$
$$y_i = y_i^* (1 + \zeta_i).$$

Substituting these expressions into the previous system and excluding the square terms we obtain

$$\frac{d\epsilon_i}{dt} = \sum_j \alpha_{ij}x_j^*\epsilon_j + \sum_j \beta_{ij}y_j^*\zeta_j$$

$$\frac{d\zeta_i}{dt} = \sum_j \gamma_{ij}x_j^*\epsilon_j + \sum_j \delta_{ij}y_j^*\zeta_j$$

Now, if the partitioned urban interaction matrix has all its diagonal elements zero, i.e. $\alpha_{ii} = \delta_{ii} = 0$, then this matrix is

$$A = \left[\begin{array}{c|c} A^{11} & A^{12} \\ \hline A^{21} & A^{22} \end{array} \right],$$

$$A_{11}^{11} = \|\alpha_{ij}x_j^*\|, A^{12} = \|\beta_{ij}y_j^*\|, A^{21} = \|\gamma_{ij}x_j^*\|, A^{22} = \|\delta_{ij}y_j^*\|,$$

so that the sum of its eigenvalues, the trace of A, is zero. In turn this requires that either at least one eigenvalue has positive real part, or all eigenvalues be pure imaginary. The end-result is that the system is either neutrally stable (centre-type equilibrium with periodic motion) or divergent (source). This in turn implies that if the urban system has an equilibrium configuration then this equilibrium is unstable or neutrally stable. Slight perturbations of the urban ecological system will result in either one or more cities becoming extinct, or one or more cities growing beyond any limit set on size, over extended time-horizons (Appendix V).

What if the diagonal elements are not zero (or their sum equal to zero)? Gardner and Ashby (1970), have looked at the properties of relatively large ecosystems whose species are randomly connected. Their conclusions, based on computer simulations, reveal that these systems seem to exhibit stable behaviour up to some level of connectance and beyond these levels they become unstable (May, 1973, p. 63).

May (1971) analytically derived the criterion for stability in the case of random connectance. His results can be directly transferred to the urban ecosystem. The connectance of the urban system C is the probability that any pair of cities (either through their population size or their reward levels) will interact. It is the percentage of non-zero elements in the urban matrix A. The rest, $1-C$, will be zero. Each non-zero element is assumed equally likely to be positive or negative so that one can assume it to be drawn from a distribution of random numbers with mean zero and standard deviation s. This s expresses the average interaction magnitude. May then asks the question: what is the probability that such a randomly drawn connectance C with interaction magnitude s corresponds to a stable system? He shows that the probability P tends to one (May 1981, ch. 10),

$$P(2I, C, s) \to 1$$

as: $\eta = s(2IC)^{1/2} < 1$; and $P \to 0$ if $\eta > 1$. The transition from stability to instability is rather sudden when the number of towns I is very large ($I \gg 1$), or the connectance C, or the average strength of interaction s among cities exceed critical values. Thus, stable urban systems comprise small numbers of cities, or cities weak in connectance, or with low average strength of interaction.

There are a few further conclusions that can be drawn from the above analysis; if a number of urban areas have a stable equilibrium, then as I or the connectance of the system increases the average number of cities compatible with stability properties declines. If large and richly connected cities are stable, this is only because the connections among them are highly non-random.

An urban ecosystem with randomly chosen interactions is unlikely to be stable if I is large. If n new towns are introduced in an existing stable system the result could be either that the new towns will decay to extinction or some existing towns will be eliminated if the original I

is close to a critical threshold; or the n new towns will gradually move towards their steady state, if I is below the critical threshold. Both results hinge upon the strength of the interconnectance.

Now the analysis switches to relative growth urban models. At first, only population growth models will be analysed. In Part I, B.1. mention was made of the Volterra conservative systems.

$$\dot{x}_i = x_i F_i; \quad i = 1, 2, \ldots, I$$

where F_i are linear functions of x_i with coefficients a_{ij}, satisfying the conservation condition

$$\sum_i \sum_j a_{ij} x_i x_j = 0.$$

In urban ecology a different condition is of interest, namely

$$\sum_i x_i = 1.0$$

so that relative redistributions are focused upon. By assuming the latter, the Volterra condition is derived, Sonis (1983), but the Volterra conservation condition does not imply the urban one. Volterra's conservation condition results from a variation of an original quantity V,

$$V = \sum_i \alpha_i x_i.$$

This is a more general expression than the urban conservation condition where $\alpha_i = 1$ $(i = 1, 2, \ldots, I)$ and

$$V = \sum_i x_i = 1.$$

Still, the multiple-cities urban community matrix must be anti-symmetric with zero diagonal elements for steady state to exist. These conditions, however, do not imply that the original interaction coefficients must be equal with opposite signs for two species, or that externalities (the friction coefficient) must be zero. Because of the substitution for one of the populations from the conservation condition

$$x_{i^o} = 1 - \sum_{\substack{i=1 \\ i \neq i^o}} x_i$$

these properties must apply to a transformed matrix.

Thus, the trade-off in generality frees the analyst from the requirement that an odd or even number of species dictate the existence of the equilibrium.† It can also allow the analyst to derive the governing least effort integral following Volterra (see last part of Appendix III for the case of conservative systems). However, due to the inability in obtaining closed-form solutions to the system of differential equations, far from equilibrium the urban conservation condition might be violated.

Empirical evidence clearly demonstrates that the urban sector of a nation over a time-span of a century or so obeys patterns which are consistent with stability properties of dynamical ecological systems; namely, the overwhelming majority of US cities' relative population and per capita income studied over the period 1890–1980 seem to be adequately described by spiral sinks. There are instances in which, while at their steady state, some mature cities experience some sudden shifts (abrupt declines in population and income accumulation). However, it is speculated that these shifts are the result of perturbations displacing the original steady state to a new position so that new spiral sink motions are in progress. No divergent movements have been observed so that city size would seem to be exponentially driven towards exceeding certain limits; or that its average reward function has been continuously diverging at accelerating motion from reasonable levels.

Given the above, a number of conclusions are drawn. The model by which one is to replicate the dynamic behaviour of inter-urban ecology must be such that stability is its dominant feature. Since only small-scale models are consistent with such stability properties, the urban web of a nation or region must be of small dimensionality. This implies that, first, an urban setting must be strongly connected to only a small number of other settings or to a well-defined environment; and second, that large-scale models are inappropriate tools to model the aggregate behaviour or an urban setting operating within a nation or a region. Since the inter-city links are highly non-random, one could attribute this to possible strong hierarchical linkages found in the urban sector of a nation. Whether or not these hierarchies are regional (so that there are strong intra-regional inter-urban and weak inter-regional links, or that the strong inter-urban links cut across regions) is still an open question. Central place theory has suggested that cities form hierarchies regionally structured and these hierarchies are manifested through some regularities in city size distributions. These hierarchies could possibly be viewed

† The multiple-cities relative dynamics are more fully explored by D. Dendrinos and M. Sonis (1984).

as stability factors in the inter-urban structure of a nation. This is developed further in Section H of this Part. Since cities do become extinct over centuries of urban evolution, one must expect that inter-connectance increases, if May's result is to apply over such extensive time-horizons.

A note on the case of population and income growth and inter-actions. There are two independent conservation conditions, one on population and one on income. The Volterra potential, integral, and interpretations are no longer applicable. In the transformed (after suitable substitution) matrix of community interaction, the elements are not anti-symmetric and the diagonals are not zero. The May complexity vs. stability arguments for absolute growth still apply. However, according to this argument, a city may be driven to income or popu-lation extinction but not necessarily together. These could, indeed, be pathological cases.

An extension of the urban Volterra–Lotka model which is of interest in view of the previous discussion on complexity vs. stability is that of incorporating different income groups into the model. This can be done by considering an average factor reward for different groups prevailing nation-wide and a different carrying capacity by income group for each town. Within such a framework, one can study the conditions under which income groups integrate or aggregate in an inter-urban context.

2. Multiple populations urban models: some results from Volterra

The dissipative Volterra systems produce results directly transferable to urban absolute growth models with population–income interaction; and to the urban relative growth in population, only, models with dissipative terms. Some of the general Volterra results will now be reviewed. Stronger conclusions can be drawn through the use of a more specific theorem. An earlier result by Volterra (1926, pt. 3) on some dynamic models with functions

$$\dot{z}_1 = z_1 (a_1 - \sum_k b_{1k} z_k)$$

where certain additional conditions are satisfied, are pertinent to the urban ecological construct. The general solution of a system of inter-acting towns like the above is

$$z_1(t) = z_1(0) \exp \int_0^t (a_1 - \sum_k b_{1k}^{\bullet} z_k) \mathrm{d}t.$$

Let α_1 be positive numbers so that

$$F = \sum_1 \sum_k \alpha_1 b_{1k} z_k z_1 .$$

The Volterra theorem says that if F is positive definite there exists a limit $\bar{Z}$ for all the z's. It can be extended to say that if F is positive definite there exists a number X and a number Y such that none of the urban settings' population and income can exceed these limits correspondingly from a certain time on. The proof can be found in Appendix VI. This has certain implications, not only for primate cities in developing nations where concern for growth is strong, but for cities in developed nations like the US. As it was shown empirically that US metropolitan areas' population and income vary within limits, assuming positive definiteness of the quadratic term is not unreasonable. It also can be concluded that, at least for the US, the upper limits on x and y are not very high; in the case of normalized population size this is at the vicinity of 70×10^{-3} and for an urban per capita income ratio to that of the average prevailing in the US is about 1.40.

A corollary to the above is that if one of the metropolitan areas of a region or nation has a positive growth rate (in either income or population) then the metropolitan association will be stable; it is impossible for the entire urban sector to become extinct if the equilibrium is perturbed and none of the urban settings can increase without bounds. Further, the variation in a single city's population or income will exhibit damped oscillations, so that the metropolitan system will tend towards its equilibrium state. This is exactly what the empirical investigation into the US metropolitan areas revealed.

Some further results will be mentioned here without proof. They draw from Volterra (1926, pt. 3). If in a dissipative metropolitan association of I cities an equilibrium exists for a set of I cities an equilibrium exists for a set of I-J towns; and if the growth rates of the remaining J towns (either in population or income) are negative at the equilibrium point; then the small variations of the entire metropolitan association result from superimposing the variation between positive limits (in either population or reward) of the I-J cities on a decline in all cities. Eventually the variation leads to a monotonic decrease to extinction of the first J cities and to variations of the remaining I-J metropolitan areas in a neighbourhood of their equilibrium state.

The addition of a new town of sufficient size or income could disturb the equilibrium state of a given urban ecological association irreparably. This is possibly the state of affairs in developing nations with the introduction of a very high income-generating capacity in the capital city. This city will drive to extinction a number of cities until stability is obtained in the urban system of the nation or region. If on the other hand the new town is small enough within the urban ecological association, the resulting small variation of the whole urban association will lead towards extinction of the new city: the new town is a slight perturbation which eventually will die out. All these conclusions are drawn based on earlier theorems by Volterra on general dissipative ecological associations.

Some even stronger statements can be derived from a more restrictive assumption. It can be shown that under particular conditions it is possible in the very long run to have the whole urban system of a nation collapsing to a single town (Appendix VII). This singularity, however, necessitates that the urban ecological system reaches some rather isolated areas of the landscape of geographies and thus it must be a very rare historical event.

3. N-species ecology and general equilibrium in economics

In view of the complexity/stability properties of the ecological community matrix pointed out by May, some implications probing large dimensionality in general competitive equilibrium theory in economics become of interest. The general equilibrium model, formulated originally by Walras, for competitive markets is (see Henderson and Quandt, 1971)

$$Q_j = \sum_i Q_{ij}(p_1, p_2, \ldots, p_J)$$

where Q_j is the total excess demand of commodity j ($j = 1, 2, \ldots, J$) and Q_{ij} is the excess demand for commodity j by consumer i, and p_j is the price of commodity j. The condition is stated in terms of prices; it could also be stated in terms of quantities. Aggregate excess demand at all times must be zero:

$$Q_j(p_j, j \in J) = 0 \quad j = 1, \ldots J.$$

Walras's law states that, given budget constraints (linear functions of prices) for all consuming agents for all commodities, then

$$\sum_i \sum_j p_j Q_{ij} = \sum_j p_j Q_j = 0$$

since $Q_j = \sum_i Q_{ij}$. Multimarket competitive equilibrium is fully described by the J equations with J unknown prices. One of these equations is redundant. The unique solution, if it does exist, is an array of prices p_j^* expressed as a ratio to a numeraire price. Existence of a solution requires that its Jacobian does not vanish at a small neighbourhood. This system has been extensively examined in mathematical economics and not much will be added here.

If the general system is reformulated to a general disequilibrium system so that in general

$$\sum_j p_j Q_j \neq 0$$

becoming equal to zero only at equilibrium, and

$$\dot{p}_j = p_j \sum_m p_m Q_m$$

where Q_m is a function of quantities $q_m - q_m^o$, where q_m^o are initial endowments, then the general market disequilibrium system becomes equivalent to the general Volterra–Lotka system. The above redefinition implies disequilibrium consumer and firm behaviour. This may not be a very interesting extension, however. A much richer one seems to be the following statement of the general dynamic disequilibrium formulation

$$\dot{p}_j = p_j \sum_m p_m Q_m^j$$

where Q_m^j is quantity demand from sector j by sector m. Quantities Q_m^j are assumed in this model to be fixed parameters (slow variables), whereas prices p are the fast adjustors. At equilibrium:

$$\dot{p}_j = p_j^* \sum_m p_m^* Q_m^j = 0$$

so that a set of non-zero equilibrium prices p_j^* exists, if

$$\sum_m p_j^* Q_m^j = 0 \quad j = 1, 2, \ldots, I$$

The $p_j^* Q_m^j$ entries constitute the community interaction matrix of ecology. Note that the diagonal elements are $2p_j^* Q_j^j$. This is the simplest case. One now can transfer all statements regarding complexity and stability in ecology to complexity and stability in multimarket competitive disequilibrium in economics. Of course, the most important aspect of such a transfer is that since there are abundant cross-effects in a large enough number of markets, the multi-commodities model cannot be in dynamic equilibrium for all commodities: some become extinct and/or others dominate in quantity. Prices may also fluctuate in a non-convergent manner. Both are widely observed phenomena.

G. DYNAMIC STABILITY OF AGGREGATE URBAN CAPITAL ACCUMULATION

In this section introduction of capital into the urban ecology is attempted. Section G.1 employs capital formation (accumulation/depletion) in the urban Volterra–Lotka model. Section G.2 shows how the May results on chaotic behaviour can be met by the capital formation process in a mathematical economic framework.

1. Capital formation in the urban ecological model

Until now the urban economy was modelled as if two sectors were sufficient to describe its dynamics. Relative population and its reward accumulations were modelled by two Volterra–Lotka-type kinetic equations, which provided the economic landscape of an aggregate urban economy operating within a national or regional environment. Use was made of the observation that relative growth dynamics of urban areas seem to be stable within time-spans of approximately 100 years. It was deduced that the connectance among many urban settings of a regional economy must be highly non-random and each setting must be selective in its interdependencies with the environment. Further, a small number of equations (and sectors) were found empirically to be sufficient in describing the dynamic properties of an aggregate urban economy.

Urban areas contain, however, another ubiquitous element, namely built capital stock. Its properties have been well identified in capital formation theory: it accumulates in lumps, it depreciates; it is characterized by locational fixity, durability, and indivisibility. Over relatively short time-spans it exhibits dynamic stability in the sense that oscillations in the magnitude of construction/destruction activity in urban settings have diminishing amplitudes as a function of time. A state of intensive construction levels is succeeded by a state characterized by lack of any construction over relatively prolonged time-periods. Perturbations of the urban economy may shift the capital accumulation damping motion to a different attractor similarly to the population–reward case described earlier.

If one wishes to examine the relative (normalized over a regional or national average) accumulation process of the capital stock in reference to the other two urban accumulations (population and its reward factor) then a third kinetic equation can be incorporated within the same dynamic framework, under particular specifications. Starting with a rather broad statement of the problem for a particular open city one can postulate

$$\dot{x} = xF_1(x,y,z)$$
$$\dot{y} = yF_2(x,y,z)$$
$$\dot{z} = zF_3(x,y,z)$$

where the third simultaneous differential equation describes the net investment (disinvestment) at time period t normalized over a national or regional quantity. The functions F depict appropriate inter-urban driving differentials (being functions of various carrying capacities and regional averages).

In contrast to the neo-classical economic growth theory, for example Solow (1970), the urban ecological framework depicts urban capital accumulation in relative terms within an effective environment the specific urban area operates. As a result, aggregate production and capital accumulation functions are not necessary, since within the ecological framework it is not necessary to obtain the absolute quantity of output produced and capital investment made within a particular town.

Turning now to the dynamic stability conditions of the three-sector urban ecological model, first, linear functions F in their three arguments (the simplest form) will be analysed

$$\dot{x} = (a_1 + a_{11}x + a_{12}y + a_{13}z)x$$
$$\dot{y} = (a_2 + a_{21}x + a_{22}y + a_{23}z)y$$
$$\dot{z} = (a_3 + a_{31}x + a_{32}y + a_{33}z)z.$$

The above specification contains all possible expanded forms of the linear formulations as the parameters vary from $-\infty$ to $+\infty$. In matrix notation, for every town

$$\frac{\dot{x}}{x} = Ax + \bar{a}$$

where x is the vector of the three urban economic variables and $A = \| a_{ij} \|$ is the expanded urban matrix, and $a = \| a_i \|$ is the vector of independent growth rates. Linearizing around the equilibrium point and forming the expanded urban Jacobian matrix one obtains

$$J = \begin{bmatrix} a_{11}x^* & a_{12}x^* & a_{13}x^* \\ a_{21}y^* & a_{22}y^* & a_{23}y^* \\ a_{31}z^* & a_{32}z^* & a_{33}z^* \end{bmatrix}$$

The solutions of the expanded linearized urban economic system are

$$x(t) = \sum_{j=1}^{3} C_{1j} \exp (\lambda_1 t)$$

$$y(t) = \sum_{j=1}^{3} C_{2j} \exp (\lambda_2 t)$$

$$z(t) = \sum_{j=1}^{3} C_{3j} \exp (\lambda_3 t)$$

with C_{ij} being constants depending on the starting points for x, y, and z; and λ_i are the three eigenvalues of the system's characteristic polynomial given by

$$(J - \lambda I) x(t) = 0$$

with J being the 3×3 urban Jacobian and I the identity matrix. The eigenvalues are all not zero if the determinant vanishes

$$\det |J - \lambda I| = 0.$$

If one eigenvalue has a positive real part then the whole system is unstable (since one variable will grow continuously in an exponential manner). On the other hand, if all eigenvalues have negative real parts then the system is stable. Neutral stability results when one eigenvalue has a zero real part and the rest have negative real parts.

There are necessary conditions, given by the Routh-Hurwitz stability criterion which, if all satisfied, result in the eigenvalues of the characteristic polynomial to possess negative real parts and thus the expanded urban economic system to be stable. These conditions are for this problem as follows

$\cdot\, a_{jj} \leqslant 0$ for all $j = 1, 2, 3$

$\cdot\, a_{jj} \neq 0$ for at least one j

$\cdot\, a_{ij}a_{ji} \leqslant 0$ for all $j \neq i$ $(i,j = 1, 2, 3)$

$\cdot\, \det J \neq 0.$

If at least one of the above conditions does not hold then the sytem is either stable or unstable depending on the magnitude of the coefficients. The first condition requires that there are no external positive economies of agglomeration in the three accumulating variables (population, output/income/reward, and capital stock). The second condition implies that in at least one sector there are negative economies of agglomeration (the stabilizing factor). The third condition is of major interest: it requires predation between all pairs of variables; so that symbiotic $(+ +)$ or purely competitive $(- -)$ conditions in any pair of sectors of an aggregate urban economy, it is concluded, can produce instability: stability requires that one variable increases continuously at the expense of another. The final requirement that the determinant be non-singular guarantees real-value solutions to the system.

Introduction of the capital sector does not disturb the dynamic stability of the aggregate population accumulation process, or in other words, the presence of the capital cycle does not impose undamped oscillations upon the population stock, at least when capital and population accumulations are of the predatory type. This is a conclusion of some potential interest to Marxist analysis. The number of parameters along which the urban landscape is now defined has grown to six, whereas in the single-city two-sector urban model the number of key parameters was two. The area of the landscape where instability settles in is relatively larger now: the chances for instability have grown exponentially.

If the capital sector of an urban setting exhibits stability it must be concluded that the particular conditions guaranteeing dynamic stability characterize the expanded three-sector urban economy. The counter-intuitive result of the above analysis is that when capital is considered together with income and population, the likelihood of the system being unstable increases. One would expect capital formation to be a stabilizing force, at least in the short run. If so, then its connectivity with population and income must be highly selective.

If any of the F functions is of second degree in any of the three arguments then the isoclines contain fold-type catastrophes with the

stable part of the fold composed of sinks and the unstable part of
saddles. A third-degree function F, in any of the three arguments (x, y, z), generates a cusp-type catastrophe; for higher-order polynomials
higher-order catastrophes result.

2. The May chaos in the neo-classical capital formation theory

For the moment a digression is made from the ecological framework,
and a purely (neo-classical) economic point of view is adopted. It can
be shown that, if viewed in isolation, the capital accumulation process
of an urban area can produce quite complicated dynamics itself. The
presence of time-lags is one source for these dynamics. Consider initially
the following production process for aggregate output

$$Q(t) = AK(t - T)^a L(t - T)^b$$

where Q is output; A is a technology coefficient; K is capital stock and
L labour. In this, constant returns to scale $(a + b = 1)$ Cobb–Douglas
production function with two input factors, T is the time-lag. Trans-
forming it to output $(q = Q/L)$ and capital $(k = K/L)$ per unit of labour,
one obtains

$$\frac{1}{A} q(t) = k(t - T)^a.$$

Now if the savings rate is n and the depreciation rate is m, then the net
capital accumulation is given by

$$\dot{k}(t) = -mk(t) + nq(t).$$

Under the (possible) condition that in certain cases it might be so that
the value of the labour savings technological coefficient is

$$A = \frac{1 - k(t - T)^a}{k(t - T)^{a-1}}$$

the neoclassical aggregate capital per unit of labour equation becomes

$$\dot{k}(t) = -mk(t) + nk(t - T) [1 - k(t - T)^a].$$

This is the form of the time-delay differential equation studied by
May (1979) which produces in certain regimes chaotic behaviour.
Whether or not this is of mere mathematical interest rather than an appropriate description of aggregate urban capital formation process is not
obvious immediately, needing data collection and empirical investigation.

In summary: formulating a capital, income, population accumulation model, indicates that stability is more likely with predatory inter-connectance. However, introduction of a third sector into the ecological model increases the chances for unstable behaviour. Utilizing a time-delay differential equation for capital accumulation employing a neo-classical economic framework, and by using a result by May, it was found that capital accumulation can produce patterns seemingly chaotic for particular values of capital productivity. Thus, if the assumption regarding stable inter-urban ecologies holds, it must imply that capital formation must be a process operating far from unstable domains of the urban landscape.

H. URBAN ECOLOGICAL DIVERSITY

In this section the focus is on subjects of diversity and urban differentiation, and their underlying stability properties. An urban model of diversity is proposed based on entropic formulation, first. Then the model is used to establish urban hierarchies and model the connections among urban settings within such hierarchies. An attempt to reformulate central place theory (Berry, 1967) is made, in a dynamic mode.

1. The entropy of an urban hierarchy

A great deal of work has surrounded the area of ecological diversity in theoretical ecology. Mostly of a statistical nature, this work attempts to derive testable hypotheses regarding laws of community composition. Although the value of such a theory in general ecology is not clear at this stage, because of the widespread interest regarding information theory in the field of urban and regional science and geography, see Wilson (1970) and others, this subject will be briefly reviewed and some extensions will be made regarding its potential use in dynamic urban ecology. The construction of an urban hierarchy in particular will be linked to the topic of diversity.

Based on Shannon's information theory entropy index H (Shannon and Weaver, 1949), with p_i being the probability of occurrence of (mutually exclusive among elements in a set I) event i

$$H = - \sum_i p_i \log p_i$$

$$\sum_i p_i = 1.0$$

a number of indices have been proposed to measure ecological diversity. Simpson (1949) suggests the following index

$$H = (\log \sum p_i^a) / (1 - a)$$

which as $a \rightarrow 1$ becomes Shannon's index. This particular index is argued for on the basis of capturing an indication of concentration or 'dominance' in a multiple species ecological community. The dominance is measured by the quantity

$$\sum_i p_i^a.$$

An alternative index proposed originally by Brillouin (1962) is the following measure

$$H = \frac{1}{x} \log \frac{X!}{\prod\limits_i x_i!}$$

$$\sum_i x_i = X; \quad (i = 1, 2, \ldots, I).$$

This index resembles the Wilson maximum entropy formulation objective function of spatial interaction models. A fuller discussion of the ecological implications of these indices can be found in Pielou (1975). Both the Simpson and Brillouin indices contain the three basic properties of the Shannon index. For a given I the maximum H is obtained when $x_i = 1/I$. Given two sets with identical total populations, but with I and $I + 1$ elements used to classify the populations in a mutually exclusive fashion, the set with $I + 1$ elements has a higher H. Finally, the entropy of multiple (not necessarily independent) classifications of a given set is the sum of all upper-level weighted entropies down to the lowest level classification.

The third property has been used by Pielou to derive an index of hierarchical diversity in a community when the taxonomic composition of the communities varies. If two communities with the same number of species but different number of genera are sampled Pielou argues that the one with the higher number of genera has a higher diversification index. This is true for the metropolitan structure of a region where the level of biological genera and species is equivalent to the different levels of SIC code disaggregation. Two cities with the same number of industrial employment types at fourth-digit SIC but different number of employment types at the first-digit SIC composition must have different diversification indices.

Assume a hierarchical breakdown of a metropolitan area's industrial bases at K levels of hierarchical decomposition, with J_k elements in each. Then the Shannon index of entropy can give the following breakdown of metropolitan industrial diversification

$$H(K, K-1, \ldots 1) = H(K) + H_K(K-1) + H_{K, K-1}(K-2)$$

$$+ H_{K, K-1, \ldots, 2}(1)$$

where the last level contains all industries I. At any intermediate level n the weighted index of diversification is

$$H_{K, K-1, \ldots K-n}(K-n-1) = \sum_{j=1}^{J_{K-n-1}} z(K-n, K-n-1)$$

$$\ln z_{K-n}(K-n-1)$$

with $z(K-n, K-n-1)$ being the joint probability of events $K-n$ and $K-n-1$ and $z_{K-n}(K-n-1)$ being the conditional probability so that

$$z_{K-n}(K-n-1) = \frac{z(K-n, K-n-1)}{\sum_j z(K-n, K-n-1)}; \quad j = 1, 2, \ldots, J_{K-n-1}.$$

Why is an index of diversification useful in urban ecological analysis? The answer to this question may not be immediately obvious. An hierarchical decomposition of the metropolitan sector of a region can be constructed based on the level of diversification of its constituent cities. This hierarchical diversity may provide some indication of vitality within the region. Jacobs (1969) places a heavy emphasis upon the role of diversification of the industrial base of a metropolitan economy on the growth or decline patterns of the city. Such links may exist at the regional level as well. More empirical work is needed along these lines, however, for such connections to be made. Evidence at the metropolitan level seems to indicate that specialization of an urban industrial base provides the initial push for growth, with sustained growth over the medium range (20-30 years) maintained only when relative diversification of the city's industrial base is attained. This was evident from the Denver and Pittsburgh SMSAs (see Table II.5). Denver's rapid economic growth in the past forty years followed this prescription, whereas Pittsburgh's continuous decline followed a failure to diversify.

TABLE II.5.   *Diversification*[1] *index and share of US population for Pittsburgh and Denver: 1940-70*

Pittsburgh	H[2]	P[3]
1940	.9296	1570.2
1950	.9099	1453.3
1960	.8815	1326.8
1970	.9583	1171.9
Denver		
1940	.9588	339.0
1950	.9840	404.5
1960	.9753	515.8
1970	1.0456	605.2

[1] The index is computed for the one-digit SIC code (nine industries)
[2] The diversification index is computed according to the Shannon formula for each SMSA and the US; the indicated number is the ratio of the two
[3] The SMSA population share is $x10^{-5}$ of US total population

2. An alternative to central place theory urban nesting system

Assume that a clustering of cities is derived on the basis of their industrial diversification index H vertically, so that cities with lower H lie higher in the nesting and urban areas with higher H lie below. Cities would also be grouped horizontally, so that cities with relatively similar industrial composition would belong to the same group. In the US these groups could be classified as agriculture-related, mining-related, heavy manufacturing, and electronics-related industries for example.

In Fig. II.8, a proposed nesting is schematically shown. The very top includes all rural areas which export agricultural products and natural resources. Next, clusters of cities with relatively low industrial diversification indices are included, and so on. A_1 and A_2 represent different basic industrial groups. Each box includes the cluster of metropolitan areas belonging to this classification. Thus, x is total employment (or population) of all cities in the cluster.

Interaction among the various clusters of cities can be captured by the following system of differential equations depicting a variety of geographies connecting each pair of clusters

$$\dot{x}_{ij} = x_{ij}F(x_{ij}; \; i\epsilon I; \; j\epsilon J)$$

where i is an index of diversification ($i = 1, 2, 3$); and j denotes industrial class ($j = 1$, 2 in the example of Fig. II.8). A particular specification of the above system employing only a vertical breakdown is the plant-herbivorous-carnivorous ecological system by Volterra (1926, pt. III); and the four-level system of resource, prey, intermediate predators, top predators by Smith (1974), Watt (1969), and others.

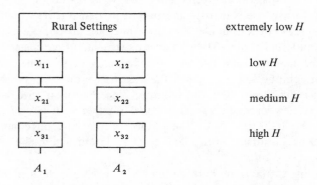

FIG. II.8. *An urban clustering scheme*
It is constructed on the basis of an industrial diversification
index (H) and an industrial classification type (A)

These interactions are interesting because, in the general ecological theory, they produce through a variety of interconnectances different stability properties for the simulated system. Volterra, for example, shows under what conditions the plant and herbivorous population will be able to sustain a carnivorous population. Smith reports, using particular specifications denoting predatory- and competitive-type ecologies among six species, through numerical analysis that

(a) competition at the first level (among prey for resources) results in destabilizing the system;
(b) competition among generalist (top) predators is stabilizing;
(c) competition at the intermediate levels (among specialist predators) produces inconclusive results upon the system's stability.

Predation, as it was discussed earlier, is the main urban ecological connectance and there is no reason to believe that at a more aggregative level than the single city things are different. As in the clusters of Fig. II.8, the x_{ij}'s are sums of urban population (or employment), one must expect equivalent (although not identical) conclusions to be drawn from the urban hierarchical system, as well, to these drawn by

Smith. The study of such urban hierarchical systems could be the subject of future work.

3. *Evolution of the urban hierarchy*

The most promising use of the literature on diversity and clustering seems to be in the area of urban evolution. A basic feature of the urban hierarchical structure is that the location of particular cities within the hierarchy does not remain constant over time, but instead can change, at times quite drastically. These sudden movements of particular cities within the hierarchy are tied into the dynamics of the urban area's industrial composition. Changes in the industrial production processes and/or output imply that the industrial decomposition (SIC code) changes as new products appear expanding either vertically or horizontally the industrial base. The change of the base underlies the development of urban settings and their evolution within the urban hierarchical structure.

According to the framework outlined earlier within which an urban hierarchy is formed one might see the dynamics of the urban hierarchy develop as follows: each city's function (industrial composition, i.e. diversification) expands or contracts either by introduction or depletion of already existing industrial activity; or by introduction of new industrial activity through technological innovation. This will shift downwards the location of an urban area in Table II.4.

Adoption of a new industrial production process (either in the production of an existing commodity, or the introduction of a new product altogether) follows the concept of Fig. II.1 and II.2. The vertical axis represents an index of return (relative price) for the technology or the product. A number of alternative new production techniques and/or new commodities compete for adoption at any particular urban area. As long as the demand curve does not intersect the supply curve the new technology/product does not materialize. As these curves shift over time the tangency point is reached for some of them, implying that at this locale the new technology or product can then be introduced.

One might speculate that new processes and/or products originate at the bottom of the hierarchical structure of Table II.4 where the diversification index is the highest (Jacobs, 1969). Obsolescence of the capital stock, none the less, might result in an upward movement toward higher levels of specialization at later stages of an urban area's dynamics. Similarly, at an earlier stage, the introduction of a new product might also sufficiently dominate a particular urban economy so as to push it upward, too. In all likelihood the motion of an urban area within the hierarchical scheme proposed is not unidirectional but instead could be of an oscillatory nature.

Finally, one can say a few words about the industry-based nature of urban cycles. If the above-mentioned relationship between industrial base and urban location in the hierarchy does hold, then one could possibly describe urban cycles at a given level of the hierarchy as the result of broader cycles in the national economy. These cycles are tied in with particular behaviour of major industries' cycles. One can depict such behaviour in their relative performance in the stock market. Cities may exhibit more frequent motions the more sensitive they are to (when specializing in) such cyclical industries.

I. OPTIMUM URBAN ECOLOGY

This section summarizes a few results from an optimum formulation of the urban Volterra–Lotka System. It further supplies some comments on the substance of such a formulation within an urban context. Although the issue of optimum urban diversification and hierarchies dynamics is potentially very fruitful, it is not addressed here.

In the case of a single open city aggregate dynamics with factor reward and population expressed in absolute values, one could employ well-established management-type models from mathematical ecology, for example Goh (1969). Models for optimum pest control, maximum yield etc. have their equivalent for absolute growth urban ecological models.

A substantive difference between the two areas of optimum growth is that, whereas in mathematical ecology management is external, in the urban field management and optimum control could be internal. Optimum control of the urban ecology along the lines of the aggregate model presented here in the case of absolute growth can occur when the income level is regulated through some tax/subsidy policy; or when congestion relief investments are made affecting the coefficient of friction and/or the urban carrying capacity level. In Dendrinos and Mullally (1983), a hypothetical set of optimum control problems were solved in a Volterra–Lotka framework of an urban ecological model. The optimum control strategies were found to be bang-bang type switches between applying the maximum, feasible levels of the control instruments (tax rates and public investment in congestion relief) and switching them off completely. Such erratic behaviour of urban governance is not totally removed from reality.

Optimum management of urban systems under absolute growth conditions lends itself to the use of a variety of optimizing objective functions. An objective function of pertinence is to minimize the amount of time it takes to reach the steady state from the original perturbation (starting-point). Another objective may be to maximize the total income accumulated over a time-horizon, or to minimize the social costs (friction) accumulated over a time-period, or a combination of all these.

Within a relative growth formulation, like the one presented in the previous sections, where the normalized (relative) population and per capita income levels are considered with respect to an environment (in this case the national economy), optimum control may not make a lot of sense from a local level (or even a national perspective). Since there are jurisdictional incongruities involved, at least in market economies where migration and endogenous growth are not centrally decided, an optimum growth framework is not implementable.

Optimum control urban ecological problems present another conceptual difficulty, as well. In an ecological framework the coefficients of the urban community matrix are interpreted as the collective actions of all interacting units (including governments) in a multiplicity of decision-making. Thus optimum management cannot be conceived from inside this community. If optimum control is information introduced to an ecological system externally, then the question is what is their exogenous source? This question, in reference to the subject of selection in urban ecology, is discussed at length in Part IV.

J. CONCLUSIONS

In the previous sections the main features of a 'new urban ecology' were laid out. They consist of an urban community interaction matrix, urban taxonomies, and hierarchical structure dynamics. Two other key notions, those of urban niche and patchiness, were outlined but not elaborated upon. Urban landscapes were drawn from the urban inter-action matrix and their dynamic stability analysed at various areas of the landscape.

An inter-urban Volterra–Lotka model of a predator–prey type was proposed for relative population and factor reward growth in reference to a national economy, as the descriptor of aggregate metropolitan dynamics. Empirical evidence from US SMSAs was used to test the qualitative dynamics of the model, covering mostly a period of thirty-seven years and for particular cases ninety years. A candidate for the Hopf bifurcation switching sinks to stable limit cycles, through centres, was detected in one SMSA (Rochester). Recent evidence from data regarding Madrid and Spain over the period 1950–80 seem to suggest similar sink spiral dynamic behaviour for non-US metropolitan areas as well (Dendrinos, 1984d).

It was found that metropolitan areas exhibit stable aggregate dynamics. Most of their time is spent in a fast motion towards a steady state; this equilibrium consists of a relative population carrying capacity determined by factors endogenous as well as exogenous to a particular city. Once close to their carrying capacities cities seem to undergo drastic change, shifting them to a sink spiralling type dynamic equilibrium towards a new (lower or higher) carrying capacity. This shift is due to parameter shifting.

The case of multi-urban areas interaction was reviewed next, where reference to the work by May on complexity vs. stability was made. It was concluded that if the urban sector of a national economy is stable, it must be due to a highly non-random interconnectance pattern in the urban community interaction matrix. It was hypothesized that such a condition would be met as a result of a hierarchical structure characterizing the urban sector of a nation. An alternative hierarchical structure of metropolitan areas to the central place theory was proposed, based on their industrial composition. Ecological models which model interactions among plant, herbivorous, carnivorous species were used to point out the conditions under which stability in such hierarchy dynamics can be obtained.

Selective items of the urban ecology were also discussed. They were associated with some interesting extensions of earlier Volterra theorems on multiple species interaction. Some of these theorems were found to provide interesting insights into the dynamics of the urban sector of more and less developed nations. Aspects of optimum urban ecology were touched upon; it was pointed out that in relative aggregate urban dynamics, optimum management models may not be operational. The role of explicitly modelling, simultaneously with income and population, capital formation in urban areas upon stability was also analysed: the effect is to increase the likelihood of instability; thus, its dynamics must be restricted to particular areas of the urban economic landscape.

Finally, some connections between urban ecological theory and urban economic theory were made. The urban Volterra–Lotka model was traced to its predecessor, the strictly convex utility model of aggregate urban dynamics of urban economics. The two differential equations of the predator-prey dynamics were viewed as dynamic demand and supply conditions, i.e. price and quantity adjustments to excess conditions. Further, connections were made between the multi-species stability vs. complexity ecological model and a disequilibrium reformulation of the general equilibrium model in economics: the reformulation possibly showed why certain commodities may dominate the market, while others become extinct.

Part III.

URBAN ECOLOGY: INTRA-URBAN DYNAMICS

A. INTRODUCTION

The purpose of this section is to provide an ecologically motivated theory which describes selectively certain problems in intra-urban location. Phenomena of multiple dynamical states and bifurcating behaviour are captured, together with some aspects of dynamic instability characterizing intra-urban allocations. As in the case of inter-urban dynamics, inter-group and intra-group attraction/repulsion seem to play a key role in depicting intra-urban structure.

Continuous and sudden changes in the internal form and structure of cities have been widely recorded over short as well as longer time-spans. Widespread attention has focused on particular phenomena where change of state is present. The incidence of suburbanization in the residential and industrial production activity in North America, Western Europe, and other regions has attracted considerable interest. Slum formation and the tipping of urban neighbourhoods in relatively short time-periods from one type of residence to another are events widely documented in the US, when sudden transitions have occurred in communities of central cities from white, middle-income households to predominently black, low- to middle-income families.

A recent phenomenon, referred to as 'gentrification', whereby a transition from white to black residents at a particular neighbourhood is being reversed so that white families repossess dwellings previously owned by black households has also been recently identified in certain US metropolitan areas. It is the first indication of a seemingly cyclical movement in the residential sector by type of household.

Other dynamic changes in intra-urban form involve abrupt increases or declines in the densities of particular land uses at certain locations in the urban space at particular time-periods. Examples of such changes in the residential sector include the conversion of the built housing stock from single-family detached to rented apartment housing; or the demolition of single units and construction of high-rise condominiums. Urban land speculation and urban renewal involving attempts toward slum clearance fall under these categories of events.

Equivalent changes in employment densities are present in the industrial production activity, either by abandonment of the built structure or by conversion of the capital stock (for example, converting old warehouse buildings into service, retail establishments or residential dwellings, a recent activity underway in older sections of central business districts in the US).

All these events, and related topics, have been extensively analysed and documented in the urban literature. The purpose here is not to repeat insights gained from previous analyses, but rather to classify these phenomena within a broader class of problems examined within the context of an ecological theory, to identify the key dynamical elements these events share, and possibly to obtain certain insight into their dynamics by viewing them in reference to bifurcation theory. Specifically, the dynamic stability in the underlying circumstances giving rise to these events is the main point of interest here.

Initially, the context of intra-urban dynamics will be established and certain key problems and elements will be presented. Then, competition among land uses within an urban zone and their dynamics will be addressed. The discussion will touch the general phenomena of neighbourhood tipping, and land density–rent oscillations. A stochastic, master equation formulation of the central city–suburb, rent–density problem will be provided together with empirical evidence. This example will be used to make some major points regarding determinism and stochasticity in intra-urban structure, as well as modelling micro-foundations of macro-behaviour.

Following intra-zonal dynamics, inter-zonal interdependence will be examined and the broad class of phenomena of suburbanization/ centralization, and slum formation/preservation (rehabilitation) will be addressed. The section concludes with a general discussion of intra-urban instability in the context of the complexity vs. stability arguments due to high interconnectance.

B. INTRA-URBAN ECOLOGY AND FORM

The context of intra-urban dynamics is presented here together with certain basic definitions. In a snapshot, the various parts of an urban space are basically occupied by either or both of two activities, namely residences and industrial production. The term industrial is not to be confused with 'manufacturing', but rather it is used here in its generic sense as in the Standard Industrial Classification Code. Roads take up part of the remaining urban land, and they are considered 'intermediate' factors in the production and consumption process. Open space (not vacant land, however, which can be attributed to either residential and/or industrial use) is considered also as an intermediate factor in consumption and/or production; it can also be viewed as part of the final consumption (parks for recreation).

There are different types of residential, industrial, and intermediate (roads and open space) activities along which one can disaggregate them. Residential activity can be disaggregated according to household type, dwelling unit type, etc. Industrial use can be broken down according to the Industrial Classification Code cited earlier. Finally, there are different types of roads and parks depending upon the land utilization coefficients and/or the amount of capital improvement per unit of land. Each activity competes for a portion of the urban land and built capital stock in a given urban neighbourhood. At the same time, different locations at the urban space compete for a share of a particular activity located in the urban setting.

At a relatively higher level of activity and areal aggregation (i.e. at a more coarse scale) the land use mix is more pronounced; at the highest possible activity and areal disaggregation (i.e. the most fine scale) there are monopolies and monopsonies observed, and perfect specialization. At the same time, as one moves at finer disaggregation the relevant variables entering the analysis increase, whereas they decline at more coarse levels of resolution. At more fine levels of disaggregation data become more scarce. As a result, the desire to accommodate more categories combined with lack of data force the analyst to pick a level of disaggregation at which the theory to be tested is statistically and behaviourally optimal.

That level appropriate for intra-urban analysis is a subject for debate. It is suggested here that the ecological theory proposed below can be applied to a square-grid areal disaggregation of an urban setting with each sell the size of an average census tract. The breakdown of land use activity can follow the first digit Standard Land Use Classification Code. Along the lines found in Dendrinos (1984a) it is further asserted that there is a particular level of disaggregation which is 'generic' for a particular intra-urban ecological analysis, generic in the sense that it contains at least as many qualitative features of such dynamic ecological theory as any other *neighbouring* disaggregation. A differently motivated theory of intra-urban location could possibly be associated with a finer 'generic' areal (or activity) disaggregation. More on this topic will be presented later, particularly related to the issue of stability/instability in land use location–allocation analysis.

A basic feature of urban form is that population density (viewed as residents, workers, or trip-makers) and quantity of built capital stock per unit area of land in various uses is not uniform throughout the urban space. Further, particular types of residential and industrial activity tend to segregate over space rather than to disperse, the more so the finer the disaggregation level of the residential/industrial activity considered.

Urban environments thus are not only patchy but, further, uneven in their population and capital stock densities per unit area of land within a particular use in a particular area of the urban setting. Over space these densities vary discontinuously with discontinuities being more pronounced as the level of activity disaggregation becomes finer. Over time these densities also vary in a discontinuous manner, with the discontinuities being sharper as the unit time-period increases. Over all, land uses seem to exhibit stickiness in behaviour over time mostly due to existence of transportation and new construction/conversion of capital stock costs.

At any time-period a portion of the total quantity of a particular activity present in an urban area is allocated in differing quantities to the urban zones into which the city has been subdivided. This relative quantity level is a function of the relative net comparative advantages (example: accessibility to other zones) enjoyed in that district over other competing districts in the city by the particular land use activity considered.

Competition for location occurs among various land uses for a given district (inter-activity competition), and among various districts for a given land use (inter-zonal competition). Dynamic intra-urban location–allocation theory in an ecological framework depicts the motion of relative accumulation or depletion of land-using activities within the set of zones comprising the urban area, from an initial perturbation, on the basis of prevailing kinematic conditions. These kinetics depict dynamic interdependencies among various zones and/or land uses.

A vast body of literature exists on intra-urban theory and models, and this is not the forum to provide an extensive review. Some brief mention of key work will be indicated here. Extensive analysis has been carried out on intra-urban theoretical economic location theory, following the initial work by von Thunen (1826) and considerably extended by Beckmann (1957), Alonso (1964), Muth (1969), Mills (1972), Henderson (1977), Miyao (1981), and others. Another line of research has been the vast literature on land use and transportation models, a partial survey of which can be found in Pack (1978), originated by the highly acclaimed Lowry (1964) model. Based on gravity formulations and its extensions, the maximum entropy theory in spatial interaction models by Wilson (1970) being a notable one, these models are characterized as 'operational'. They are predominently static and equilibrium-bound in nature, although there have been exceptions (for example, the National Bureau of Economic Research Model, (Ingram *et al.*, 1972) described by its founders as of a dynamic and disequilibrium type).

Dynamic large-scale urban simulation models, quite innovative for their time, have been the Forrester (1971) urban dynamics model and the EMPIRIC model of land use (Hill, 1965). Not based on any particular theoretical foundation the Forrester model does not contain spatial disaggregation, whereas the EMPIRIC model is spatially disaggregated. A recent variation of the EMPIRIC model, although not regarded as such by its founders, is the Allen *et al.* (1978) model of intra-urban dynamics. Allen *et al.* claim that their model is motivated by a search for bifurcating points in intra-urban behaviour. The large-scale nature of the model, however, limits the analysts' ability to depict in the parameter space the points where bifurcations in the state variables occur or the nature of these bifurcations. Things are even further complicated by the fact that exogenous shocks are randomly imposed in the system of differential equations which attempts to simulate the behaviour of the urban setting.

A different approach is attempted here in modelling basic features of intra-urban ecology. The effort is made to use parsimony in devising analytic results with qualitative features that include dynamic disequilibrium, multiplicity of states, and bifurcation due to endogenous smooth variations in key parameters. There is a drawback to this endeavour. Whereas in the case of inter-urban ecological dynamics consistent data-series are available over relatively extended time-periods, this is hardly the case in intra-urban dynamics. Key inferences can be made, however, from existing commonly observed events to support particular features of a qualitative nature emerging from the theoretical construct. None the less, this is small consolation to the careful empiricist.

Inter-urban dynamics of relative metropolitan growth were found to exhibit stability properties, as demonstrated by the dominance of metropolitan areas characterized by attractor-type behaviour in reference to the national environment. It was concluded that this stability must be due to a highly non-random interconnectance prevailing among the urban areas of a nation. In contrast to this finding, the high interconnectance existing within an urban area (due to, among other factors, locational proximity) among the various activities and zones (the more so the finer the level of disaggregation analysed) must point towards inherent instability in intra-urban dynamics.

This is plainly demonstrated by two facts. First, there is widespread and significant change in intra-urban location of various activities, mostly identified by the high intra-urban residential and industrial mobility patterns found in US cities. Second, when most urban activities are considered at a fine level of disaggregation highly mixed land use patterns are not found present at most urban zones. In the US mixed land use equilibria do not exist in most zones. In a dynamic framework this may be due to the fact that certain land use activities either have become extinct at districts where an initial perturbation allowed them to start, or because locational monopolies of certain activities occurred initially in most zones. Most districts tend to specialize in land use, and most land uses tend to specialize in certain districts in cities of the US.

At a more coarse scale, however, the picture is different: there are mixed land use patterns found in most urban districts, although the dynamics of these allocations may not be always of a nodal type but instead may involve cyclical motion and oscillation. The dynamics of intra-urban location will be analysed next from an intra-zonal and inter-zonal perspective; three particular phenomena will be reviewed: gentrification, suburbanization, and slum formation.

C. INTRA-ZONAL ECOLOGY: NON-LINEAR DYNAMIC COMPETITION FOR SPACE

1. *The two-activities city; mixed land use equilibria*

In order to illustrate the basic elements of intra-urban ecology one can start by considering the case of a metropolitan area containing two activities: aggregate production and residential. These two land uses compete for land over a district of the city (to be referred to as a zone). At any time-period the zone could consist of a mixed allocation, or could be specialized in either industrial production or residential activity, or it could be vacant. The particular configuration in the zone depends on the relative advantages it enjoyed by these two activities in reference to the rest of the urban area.

Let $x_i(t)$ be the current level of normalized resident population in zone i at time t (the fraction of a city's population residing in i); and $w_i(t)$ be the current level of normalized employment in i at t. Further, let the ecological dynamics associated with the two accumulations be given by the general two species Volterra–Lotka model

$$\dot{x}_i(t) = [a_i^0 + a_i^1 x_i(t) + a_i^2 w_i(t)] \, x_i(t)$$
$$\dot{w}_i(t) = [b_i^0 + b_i^1 x_i(t) + b_i^2 w_i(t)] \, w_i(t).$$

To isolate the intra-zonal effects of competition among activities we assume here that the inter-zonal effects are minimal. In the inter-urban case of course this assumption makes sense, since what occurs in one city (in the US) does not noticeably affect the total economy. This may be questionable in the intra-urban case, where an inter- and intra-activity and zonal model may be more appropriate. Empirical evidence is required to validate either of the above assumptions, of course. For particular intra-urban phenomena, it will be seen below, the qualitative evidence seems to suggest that the assumption made in the above model produces dynamics consistent with observed patterns. Another way to formulate the problem is to assume x and w to represent the portion of the quantity of land in zone i taken up by production and residential type of land use. Thus, normalization would take place over the total amount of land available in zone i.

Exponential adjustment is assumed thus under limited growth conditions. Parameters a^0, a^1, a^2, b^0, b^1, b^2 vary (from $-\infty$ to $+\infty$) and define the intra-urban ecological landscape, so that particular values associated with a particular zone $i \in I$ (I being the total number of zones into which the urban area is subdivided) define a point in the parameter space depicting the position of zone i in the landscape. Each point in the landscape corresponds to a particular type of ecological dynamic equilibrium operating in i between resident population and production. Nations with cities which have many zones with mixed land use equilibria are not different in the dynamic structure from nations with urban areas containing mostly specialized urban zones. They are part of the same basic intra-urban ecological landscape, differing only on the location they occupy on the landscape.

In the case of intra-zonal, inter-activity ecology there are I ecological combinations for the two activities. If there are J activities to be considered, and n is the number of activities located per zone then there are

$$\binom{J}{n} = \frac{J!}{n!\,(J-n)!}$$

possible ecological connections per zone. For I zones, using the formula

$$\sum_{n=1}^{J} \binom{J}{n} = 2,$$

there are

$$I(J!) \sum_{n=1}^{J} \frac{1}{n!\,(J-n)!} = I(2^J - 1)$$

points in the intra-urban landscape which involve all possible permutation of (equal number of) activities for all zones. Apparently, an exhaustive study of all such possible ecological associations is not feasible. One must selectively study an interesting subset of these associations, preferably at dense parts of the landscape.

The two Volterra–Lotka-type differential equations define the rate of accumulation/depletion of x and w in i at t given the initial perturbation $x_i(t_0)$, $w_i(t_0)$. For the purposes of intra-urban location the initial perturbation is always close to the origin — barring large-scale developmental intervention. Accumulation/depletion in i depend upon the comparative advantages defined as differences in net rewards between i and the rest of the urban area. Net rewards could involve a discounted stream of expected net benefits over a time horizon.

A behavioural population-wide (not individual) level interpretation of the dynamics involved in the system of differential equations can be obtained by examining the signs of a^1, a^2, b^1, b^2. These signs depict the mutual effects of and on x and w near the equilibrium point(s), as well as far from equilibrium in the case at hand which involves linear isoclines. For example, when $a^1 > 0$ then net positive effects of population agglomeration are present; $a^2 < 0$ implies residential activity aversion to industrial production in i (from the residents' point of view); $b^1 > 0$ implies net benefits to industrial use from proximity to the labour force; and $b^2 > 0$ is associated with scale effects in industrial agglomeration.

Basically three types of intra-urban, intra-zonal, inter-activity ecologies can be identified following the discussion of the geographies embedded in the general Volterra–Lotka model. They are

symbiotic ecology: $a^2, b^1 > 0$
competitive ecology: $a^2, b^1 < 0$
predatory ecology: $a^2 \cdot b^1 < 0.$

Commensalism/amensalism implies that either a^2 or b^1 are equal to zero. Smooth transitions (in one parameter at a time) involve changes in the intra-urban ecology from symbiotic to predatory to competitive geographies (or vice versa) in the intra-zonal landscape. They occur through the intermediate phases of commensal and amensal geographies, according to the scheme of Table III.1. Thus, at the neighbourhood of

TABLE III.1. *Smooth transitions in geographies on the intra-urban, intra-zonal, inter-activity landscape*
Evolution due to bifurcation in intra-urban dynamics occurs at points indicated, and under additional circumstances described in the text

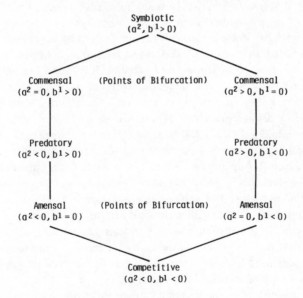

commensal and amensal areas of the landscape bifurcations occur, producing shifts in the nature of the dynamic intra-zonal, inter-activity equilibrium. Commensal and amensal geographies (among other conditions) depict critical points in the intra-zonal landscape which are associated with evolutionary changes, as the term has been used in this text. At these points one geography is transformed to another.

Zones belonging to areas of the landscape falling under these three basic categories are characterized by distinctly varying conditions. In the part of the landscape containing symbiotic intra-zonal, inter-activity ecologies only saddles and nodes occur. In the predatory landscape nodes, spirals, and saddles occur; whereas in the competitive landscape saddles and nodes describe the dynamics. The interesting question is how wide is the area on the landscape which contains the set of points corresponding to the zones of an urban setting at a particular time? In the case of inter-urban dynamics empirical evidence seems to indicate that the area is indeed very narrow and belonging to the predatory type. As it will be illustrated later, similar evidence exists for intra-urban, intra-zonal, inter-activity dynamics.

Another subject associated with the signs of the a^1, b^2 parameters in the general Volterra–Lotka model is the extent of intra-group aversion or affinity. In this case, a positive a^1 would imply that in aggregate the residential activity comprises of households which prefer higher density of their group. In case there are different types of households not willing to locate in close proximity, then a^1 must be negative.

Examining the nature of the mixed dynamic equilibria under conditions of intra-group affinity and aversion, it is found that mixed land use stable equilibria (sink nodes) are present only under intra-group aversion in symbiotic and competitive intra-urban, intra-zonal ecologies (Fig. III.1). Under predatory conditions, the incidence of mixed land use dynamic equilibria is higher and of greater variety (Fig. III.2). The analytical results which indicate the nature of the dynamic equilibria are produced in Appendix XI. Cases where stable bedroom communities or stable exclusively industrial zones emerge are numerous and can occur under almost any ecological association. Thus, it must not be surprising that they are found extensively in the US. The only exception is the case of positive intra-group effects: under any ecology type (symbiotic, predatory, or competitive) a necessary requirement for a stable specialized land use zone to exist is that a^1 and b^2 (intra-group attraction) not be simultaneously positive.

The magnitude of the parameters may vary over time, changing the shape of the part of the landscape containing the sets of points corresponding to the zones of an urban setting; it also results in each zone tracing a dynamic path over the landscape. A change in magnitude of a^2 and b^1 is associated with changes in the nature of the geographic ecology a zone belongs to, whereas changes in a^1, b^2 are associated with changes in intra-group sympathy. Finally changes in a^0, b^0 are

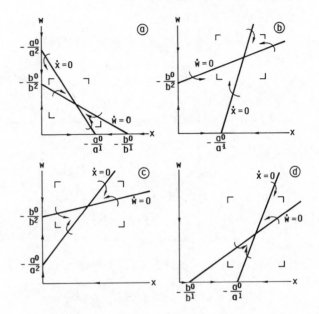

(a): competitive; $a^2, b^1 < 0; a^1, b^2 < 0, a^0, b^0 > 0, a_0/a^1 > b_0/b^1$,
$a_0/a^2 < b^0/b^2$.

(b), (c), (d): symbiotic; $a^2, b^1 > 0, a^1, b^2 < 0$.

(b): $a^0 > 0, b^0 > 0, a^1/a^2 > b^1/b^2$

(c): $a^0 < 0, b^0 > 0, a^1/a^2 > b^1/b^2, a^0/a^2 < b^0/b^2$

(d): $a^0 < 0, b^0 < 0, a^1/a^2 > b^1/b^2, a^0/a^1 > b^0/b^1$

FIG. III.1. *Cases of symbiotic and competitive stable mixed land use: intra-zonal, inter-activity equilibria in intra-urban geographies with intra-group aversion*

associated with changes induced from the zone's environment (for example, zoning changes or changes in the carrying capacities present for these activities in the zone). Apparently, variations of all the parameters must not have the same time-scales built into them. Particular phenomena recorded may provide clues as to the relative speed of change in these parameters.

2. Neighbourhood tipping and gentrification

In abstract, tipping of neighbourhoods from one land use to another over a relatively short time-span and as a result of a slight change of circumstances, initially, is a general phenomenon in intra-urban structure. It has occurred in the residential areas of central cities in the US;

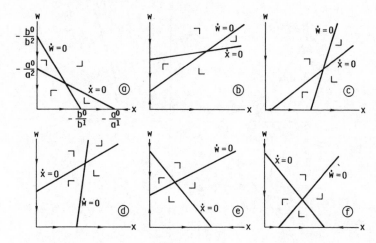

(a): $a^2 < 0, b^1 > 0; a^1 < 0, b^2 > 0, a^0 > 0, b^0 < 0, a^0/a^1 > b^0/b^1, a^0/a^2 < b^0/b^2$

(b): $a^2 < 0, b^1 > 0; a^1 > 0, b^2 < 0, a^0 > 0, b^0 > 0, a^0/a^2 > b^0/b^2, a^1/a^2 < b^1/b^2$

(c): $a^2 < 0, b^1 > 0; a^1 > 0, b^2 < 0, a^0 < 0, b^0 > 0, a^0/a^1 < b^0/b^1, a^1/a^2 < b^1/b^2$

(d): $a^2 < 0, b^1 > 0; a^1 > 0, b^2 < 0, a^0 > 0, b^0 < 0, a^1/a^2 < b^1/b^2$

(e): $a^2 < 0, b^1 > 0; a^1 < 0, b^2 < 0, a^0 > 0, b^0 > 0, a^0/a^2 > b^0/b^2$

(f): $a^2 < 0, b^1 > 0; a^1 < 0, b^2 < 0, a^0 > 0, b^0 < 0, a^0/a^1 > b^0/b^1$

FIG. III.2. *Cases of stable, predatory mixed land use: intra-zonal, inter-activity spiral equilibria in intra-urban ecology*
Only half are shown – the others can be obtained by reversing the two axes: $a^2 > 0, b^1 < 0$.

it has also occurred in industrial zones, too, where industrial expansion displaced residential uses and vice versa. Urban renewal is a case where one type of residential activity was transformed into another residential type or to an industrial use.

However, the most widely recorded empirical evidence is that of zones which at some time-period contained exclusively white middle-income households and suddenly were tipped over to non-white lower-to middle-income families. These zones were continuously losing their share of white urban population to outer city (suburban) zones. Over a relatively short time-period, the zone was converted to a different land use in a non-oscillatory manner. The qualitative features of such a transition are depicted by the phase portrait of Fig. III.3. In (a) the neighbourhood tipping phenomenon is traced in the phase portrait

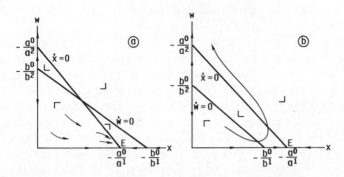

FIG. III.3. *Neighbourhood tipping and gentrification*
The change in the relative magnitude of $-a^0/a^1$ and $-b^0/b^1$ destabil-
izes the equilibrium point E. In (a) the phenomenon of tipping from w
to x is recorded; (b) depicts the phenomenon of neighbourhood reversal,
from x to w.

where the relevant trajectories are shown: a zone initially under declining share of white population (w) is tipped by a perturbation off a
path on the w-axis and it produces a motion toward point E as the zone
is increasingly occupied by non-white (x) households. The perturbation
is the result of a very small number of non-white households moving
into the zone. This is shown by the direction of the arrows in the phase
portrait of Fig. III.3(a). At the stable equilibrium E, associated with
land use specialization, the motion ceases. The zone is exclusively
occupied by households of type x.

Parameter b^0 is associated with the comparative advantages of a particular tract in reference to the urban area for use w (when $b^1 = b^2 = 0$
then $\dot{w} = -b^0 w$). As b^0 increases in absolute value, the advantages for
use w in that particular zone decrease. Changes in b^0, due to either
zoning or environmental effects (gains in comparative advantages of this
zone relative to the other zones in the metropolitan area for w) shifts
the $\dot{w} = 0$ isocline to the left. As $\dot{w} = 0$ moves beyond E, the equilibrium becomes unstable. The resulting land use configuration depicts
now a reversal to w-type households in the zone, in effect depicting the
gentrification phenomenon.

At the intra-zonal landscape this particular bifurcation in behaviour
was not associated with changes in the sign of the parameters in the
community matrix (a^1, a^2, b^1, b^2). It was simply associated with
a critical threshold in the value of b^0 relative to a^1, a^2, b^1. When
$-a^0/a^1 < -b^0/b^1$ equilibrium E was stable. However, when b^0

became large enough (in absolute terms) so that $-a^0/a^1 > -b^0/b^1$ then E became unstable.

From the above, it is clear that bifurcating behaviour is not present exclusively at points of transition in the type of intra-zonal landscape of Table III.1 (commensal, amensal). It is also present within the various landscapes, as demonstrated in the above example. Neighbourhood transition, thus, is not due to changes in inter- and/or intra-group attraction and/or repulsion exclusively, but also due to changes in the comparative advantages of a particular zone within the urban area for a particular use (in this case for w as the value of b^0 varies). Evolutionary change, associated with changes in the nature of dynamic intra-zonal equilibria, is thus found not only at the borders of the various parts of the intra-zonal landscape (a^1, a^2, b^1, b^2 approaching zero), but also in critical points within these landscapes. Both cases in Fig. III.3 result in ecological exclusion, i.e. only one activity (land use) remains in the zone.

In summary, the prevailing dynamics underlying both (a) and (b) belong to predatory ecology, with mixed intra-group attraction. They are given by the system of simultaneous differential equations

$$\dot{x} = (a^0 - a^1 x - a^2 w)x$$
$$\dot{w} = (-b^0 + b^1 x + b^2 w)w$$

where all parameters are positive. Note the community matrix: there is intra-white population sympathy and intra-non-white aversion; inter-group attraction (predation) from the white population standpoint $(+ b^1)$ and repulsion (preying) from the non-white population standpoint $(- a^2)$. It is not due necessarily to the commonly perceived notion of 'white flight' as the non-white population density increases in the zone. Within this framework, neighbourhood tipping and gentrification are viewed as a bifurcation event under predatory dynamics with mixed intra-group interaction. Smooth changes in only one parameter (b^0 here) were sufficient to reproduce gentrification. Tipping was merely due to a slight perturbation off the w-axis.

This kind of analysis may be appealing from the standpoint that *it requires a very small number of parameters to vary smoothly* in order to depict tipping and reversal in land use. It is thus suggested that the particular zones in US metropolitan settings undergoing gentrification belong to the predatory area of the intra-zonal, inter-activity landscape, and gentrification is due to changes in comparative advantages of particular zones in reference to other zones in a metropolitan area.

3. Vacant land zones and threshold in initial capital investment

It is of interest to note that zones characterized by symbiotic inter-activity ecology with positive intra-group interactions are unstable and normally result in zonal abandonment (Fig. III.4). Conditions under

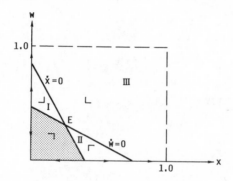

FIG. III.4. *The stable equilibrium empty zone and the minimum threshold for development: symbiotic geography* (Dashed lines denote limits)

which a zone's steady state is to remain vacant are, however, numerous in the intra-urban, intra-zonal, inter-activity landscape. Only one is shown in Fig. III.4. The dynamics are characterized by inter-group and intra-group sympathy. For real solutions to exist, the constants depicting zonal comparative advantages for each activity (a^0, b^0) must be negative (i.e. the zones must contain levels below some urban average). Equilibrium point E is a saddle. If initial intervention occurs in the shaded area of Fig. III.4 then the zone will return to a vacant land equilibrium state in a nodal fashion. If the initial perturbation falls in either areas I or II then the zone will specialize to either use. Still it contains all of the activity in the urban area. If the starting development pushes the zone in area III then the zone diversifies as well as becoming the exclusive depository of at least one of the two activities in the urban area. Such is the case in zones of relatively small urban areas. In large urban settings zoning and/or other constraints limit the extent of agglomeration or specialization.

4. *Multiple land use equilibria*

In the previous cases, the effect of x and w on each other in the vicinity of the equilibrium points and far from equilibrium were not varying because of the use of linear isoclines. However, the real effect must be the result of push–pull factors, i.e. the net outcome of some positive effects of proximity (external economics of agglomeration) and negative effects of concentration (due to externalities of density, congestion, etc.). Such conditions lead to a more realistic system containing non-linear isoclines

$$\dot{x} = (a_0 + a_1 x + a_2 x^2 + a_3 w)x, \quad (a_0, a_1, a_3 \gtrless 0, a_2 < 0)$$

$$\dot{w} = (b_0 + b_1 x + b_2 w + b_3 w^2)w, (b_0, b_1, b_2 \gtrless 0, b_3 < 0).$$

In solving the dynamics of this system the isoclines are depicted as second-degree curves, from the system of equations

$$w_1^* = -\frac{a_0}{a_3} - \frac{a_1}{a_3} x_1^* - \frac{a_2}{a_3} x_1^{*2}$$

$$x_2^* = -\frac{b_0}{b_1} - \frac{b_2}{b_0} w_1^* - \frac{b_3}{b_1} w_1^{*2}$$

where the asterisk denotes equilibrium value. The case where $a_0, a_1, a_3 > 0, a_2 < 0, b_0, b_1, b_3 > 0, b_2 < 0$ is shown in Fig. III.5: E_1 is an attractor, E_2, E_3, E_4 are saddles. For fixed values of these parameters, the land use allocation dynamics could be either of two states: one

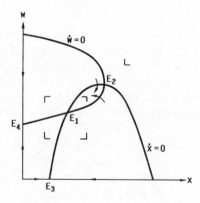

FIG. III.5.   *Intra-zonal, inter-activity mixed land use equilibria with non-linear isoclines*

stable and one unstable. As smooth variations in these parameters occur there is state switching: at the point of tangency of the two second-degree curves the stable equilibrium switches to an unstable node.

D. INTER-ZONAL ECOLOGY: NON-LINEAR DYNAMIC COMPETITION FOR URBAN ACTIVITY

1. The phenomena of suburbanization and centralization

It will be demonstrated that this phenomenon falls qualitatively in the broad class of problems identified earlier as predatory ecology with mixed intra-group attraction. The phenomenon of neighbourhood tipping in the case of intra-zonal, inter-activity ecology and the phenomena of suburbanization/centralization are methodologically equivalent. When two zones compete for one particular land use activity, for example industrial activity, the landscape of geographies can be described methodologically along the previously developed lines. There could be cases where activities will specialize in one particular zone, or where mixed zonal equilibria could result (the industrial use being split over two zones in the steady state).

Suburbanization and the movement back to the central city (in both the industrial and residential sector) point to the same type of dynamic present in the tipping and gentrification phenomena in intra-zonal ecology: predatory dynamics between suburban and central zones, i.e. mixed inter-zonal attraction, and mixed intra-zonal repulsion. Specifically, the suburbanization/centralization phenomenon can be depicted by

$$\dot{x} = (a^0 - a^1 x - a^2 w)x$$
$$\dot{w} = (-b^0 + b^1 x + b^2 w)w$$

where x is the suburban share of activity k in the metropolitan area, and w its central city share; parameters $a^0, a^1, a^2, b^0, b^1, b^2$ are positive. Predatory dynamics are present since we are in the framework of $(-+)$ landscape $(-a^2 + b^1)$ (the central city corresponding methodologically to the predator); and positive intra-central city zones interaction $(+b^2)$ coupled with negative intra-suburban zonal attraction $(-a^1)$ produce the phenomena of suburbanization and its reversal to a centralized land use pattern as b^0 varies smoothly and crosses a critical value. Given the original definition of evolutionary change the reverse movement, i.e. the decentralization to centralization phenomenon qualifies as such. It is associated with a change in the nature of the dynamic equilibrium E, of Fig. III.3, as parameter b^0 exceeds a critical level, equivalent to the case of Section C.2.

2. Slum formation and historical preservation

Slum-quality levels in the housing stock is a relative notion; it is mostly associated with older housing units with relatively depreciated capital stock. The following section attempts to supply the basic ecological ingredients of the slum formation process and its reversal, sometimes referred to as historical preservation, in a dynamic context. This places it in the class of problems already analysed, namely the neighbourhood tipping and decentralization reversal. The process of slum formation contains typical elements of patchiness and patch dynamics found in general ecology. Slum incidence is initially restricted to particular areas of an urban setting. Gradually, it tends, due to neighbourhood externalities, to spread into neighbourhood (adjacent) locations. Quality of the housing stock is an accumulating/decumulating variable. Improvement (accumulation) or deterioration (depletion) of quality level prevailing over the built capital stock of a given zone takes place through ecological interconnectance with other zones' quality level. Assume that two zones contain housing with respective average quality level stocks q_1 and q_2; assume further that the interactions between the two levels are given by the set of simultaneous differential equations

$$\dot{q}_1 = (a^0 + a^1 q_1 + a^2 q_2)q_1$$
$$\dot{q}_2 = (b^0 + b^1 q_1 + b^2 q_2)q_2$$

where the parameters vary from $-\infty$ to $+\infty$ identifying the total intra-urban quality landscape. Now, where in this landscape is the incidence of slum formation, and its reversal, dense? That is, what part of the landscape do most of the neighbourhoods within a city occupy? And what is the associated behaviour?

Before addressing these questions certain observed qualitative dynamic features of the slum formation process will be discussed. Assume that a particular zone's quality level, q_1, starts deteriorating in comparison with the prevailing quality level of the city's stock. There are two kinds of responses following this event. Neighbourhood zones experience a (slower) decline in the quality level of their stock so that there is inter-zonal affinity in terms of relative quality levels prevailing in the two zones. On the other hand, for zones that are relatively removed, spatially, from the zone undergoing slum formation, the quality level prevailing either remains constant or increases in (either absolute or) relative terms. In the following discussion only spatially separated zones will be addressed. These dynamics depict developmental change, i.e. spreading of the phenomenon of deteriorating quality level. As the focus in this Section is on an evolutionary change, namely trend reversal, the spatially remote quality interconnectance will be studied. For the purpose of this model it is assumed that slum phase is reached when the quality level attains zero level (a threshold level $\bar{q}$ is more realistic but this would not affect the results at all).

In Fig. III.6 (a) these dynamics are shown, where the arrows depict declines in the quality level of zone 1 (q_1) and increase in the quality level of the stock in the spatially separated zone 2 (q_2). E is the stable slum equilibrium. The particular specifications are

$$\dot{q}_1 = (-a^0 + a^1 q_1 + a^2 q_2)q_2$$
$$\dot{q}_2 = (b^0 - b^1 q_1 - b^2 q_2)q_2.$$

These dynamics belong to a predatory ecology ($+a^2, -b^1$) with mixed intra-group effects. The original (and older) zone undergoes slum formation when the quality level of its housing stock is positively affected by the remote (and newer) zone's quality level. The prevailing quality level in the newer zone with an increase in the relative quality of its stock, q_2, is positively affected by the deteriorating quality level of the

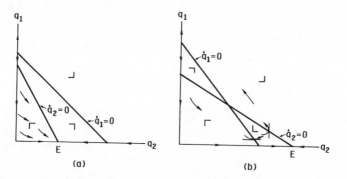

(a)   (b)

FIG. III.6. *Slum formation process and preservation.* (a) *Stable slum equilibrium;* (b) *unstable slum equilibrium and restoration*
Variables q_1 and q_2 represent average prevailing quality level in spatially separated zones 1 and 2

older zone, q_1. Thus, there are positive $(+a^2)$ and negative $(-b^1)$ spatial interconnectance (remote externalities). There is positive intra-group interaction in the zone undergoing slum switching $(+a^1)$; it implies positive quality of stock elasticity. There is negative interaction $(-b^2)$ in the high-quality level zone; it implies negative elasticity: higher quality level constitutes negative neighbourhood externality.

These two associations are at the centre of evolutionary change: they produce the (not sustained, however) cyclical movement in quality levels in spatially separated zones within metropolitan areas. The evolutionary change is triggered by parameter a^0 passing through a critical threshold (Fig. III.6 (b)) as in the case of the previous section on decentralization.

These model specifications in the slum formation process result in a stable slum equilibrium, E, so that any perturbation over a wide range of values in the (q_1, q_2) space will ultimately bring the system back to that stable slum steady state. This is of particular interest for public policy. When vast areas of the (q_1, q_2) space are such that paths lead to a stable slum the effects of relatively mild public interventions attempting to halt slum formation are bound to fail. Of key interest, none the less, are possible shifts in the $\dot{q}_1$ isocline. If a^0 increase (presumably by altering the relative location of this zone in reference to the other zones in the urban area in terms of comparative advantages — by providing higher employment accessibility, for example) these shifts may result in the isocline crossing over the stable slum equilibrium and switching it into an unstable one. This is accompanied by a reversal of the quality level dynamics (preservation/restoration). When close to this critical threshold, slight public intervention or environmental perturbation could have drastic effects.

E. SUMMARY AND GENERAL REMARKS ON INTRA-URBAN PREDATORY DYNAMICS

All previously examined cases, that of neighbourhood tipping/gentrification, suburbanization/centralization, and slum formation/restoration, are described by similar dynamic features characterizing an intra-urban ecological model of predatory-type dynamics with mixed intra-group attraction. It seems that the areas of the intra-urban ecological landscape depicting predation must be dense with zones of US metropolitan settings. It is also possible that under particular competitive conditions similar conclusions might be reached.

The six phenomena examined were shown to belong to three groups, each group containing two complémentary motions, and each motion associated with a particular urban phenomenon. All three groups were of the same dynamic ecological type, so that each phenomenon has a counterpart in a particular group. Three phenomena, historic preservation, centralization/suburbanization, and gentrification are the result of stable specialized land use equilibria transformed into unstable (source) attractors by passing through some critical value of certain model parameters. Thus, these phenomena are associated with one source of instability in intra-urban dynamics resulting from bifurcating behaviour at critical points in the intra-urban system's behaviour. As already discussed, these bifurcations are present at the border of the various types of intra-urban landscapes (at points of amensal and commensal geographies), as well as at critical points within predatory, competitive and symbiotic intra-urban, inter- (intra-) zonal, inter- (intra-) land use parts of the landscape. These critical points, where bifurcation in dynamic behaviour is recorded, are defined as points where evolutionary change is under way. Part of the class of changes associated with evolution may be leading to unstable dynamic behaviour.

Another source of intra-urban instability is due to the level of disaggregation (areal and land use activity) examined. Due to locational proximity highly patchy urban settings are randomly interconnected. The result is that the overall system in all likelihood experiences unstable type dynamics. Instability must be a fundamental property of disaggregated intra-urban dynamics, in contrast to stable inter-urban dynamical qualities. This cause for intra-urban instability is now examined in more detail.

F. INTRA-URBAN INSTABILITY, DISAGGREGATION, AND HIGH INTERCONNECTANCE

If one wishes to analyse the intra-urban ecology at a finer level of disaggregation in both land uses and areal breakdown (presumably in order to obtain higher consistency of behaviour by increasing homogeneity in agents and land features) then a different picture emerges. In contrast to the previous analysis where stability was found in aggregate intra-urban location-allocation dynamics away from critical points of bifurcation, the picture is altered when a very detailed breakdown of urban activities and zonal subdivision is examined. A relatively high degree of areal mobility among land uses is obtained by even casual empirical observations. The dynamics are characterized by a high degree of instability, where extinction and continuous growth/decline of particular zones are frequent events.

These type of dynamics are precisely depicted in a qualitative manner from ecological associations given by a Volterra–Lotka system of the form

$$\dot{x}_{k,i} = \left(\alpha_{k,i} + \sum_{k',i'} a^{k,i}_{k',i'} x_{k',i'} + \sum_{j,i'} b^{k,i}_{j,i'} w_{j,i'}\right) x_{k,i}$$

$$(i = j, \ldots I)$$

$$\dot{w}_{j,i} = \left(\beta_{j,i} + \sum_{k,i'} c^{j,i}_{k,i'} x_{k,i'} + \sum_{j',i'} d^{j,i}_{j',i'} w_{j',i'}\right) w_{j,i}$$

where $x_{k,i}$ and $w_{j,i}$ are correspondingly the levels of residential activity type k ($k = 1, 2, \ldots, K$) and industrial activity type j ($j = 1, 2, \ldots, J$). The above could be specified in either absolute or relative terms. In the case of relative growth, in addition to the above, for each activity (k and j) the total population and workers must satisfy also the conservative equations

$$\sum_i x_{k,i} = 1.00 \quad (k = 1, 2, \ldots, K)$$

$$\sum_i w_{j,i} = 1.00 \quad (j = 1, 2, \ldots, J)$$

or, if the total quantity of all uses allocated to a zone is known

$$\sum_k x_{k,i} = 1.00$$
$$(i = 1, 2, \ldots, I)$$
$$\sum_j x_{j,i} = 1.00$$

or, if only the total number of urban residents and workers are known

$$\sum_j \sum_i x_{k,i} = 1.00$$

$$\sum_j \sum_i w_{j,i} = 1.00.$$

In the absolute growth case, coefficients a, b, c, d vary from $-\infty$ to $+\infty$ and depend on a number of factors. Differences in accessibility of a particular zone (i) for a particular activity (j or k) from their respective mean city-wide value could be a significant contributor to these parameter values.

Analysis when the equilibrium x^* and w^* are non-negative is of interest. The dynamic stability properties of the various parts of this extensively disaggregated intra-urban landscape depend upon the eigenvalues of the characteristic polynomial of the linearized system with an interaction matrix

$$M = \begin{bmatrix} F_{ki} & | & F_{ji} \\ -- & + & -- \\ G_{ki} & | & G_{ji} \end{bmatrix}$$

with entries

$$f^{k,i}_{k',i'} = a^{k,i}_{k',i'} \, x^*_{k,i}$$

$$f^{k,i}_{j',i'} = b^{k,i}_{j',i'} \, x^*_{k,i}$$

$$g^{j,i}_{k',i'} = c^{j,i}_{k',i'} \, w^*_{j,i}$$

$$g^{j,i}_{j',i'} = d^{j,i}_{j',i'} \, w^*_{j,i}$$

where the dimensions of the matrix are $(K + J)I$. Stability criteria for such a matrix require that the coefficients be such that certain (increasingly involved as m becomes larger) Routh–Hurwitz conditions must be satisfied (May, 1973). Why such conditions must necessarily be met in a randomly interconnected intra-urban system is not apparent. Thus, it must be expected that, when looking at a very disaggregated level of intra-urban land use allocation patterns, chances are high that an unstable dynamic condition will be obtained. At least one of the eigenvalues of the system will have a positive real part. The areas of the very disaggregated intra-urban landscape with all eigenvalues having negative real parts are very remote, the more so the higher the activity and areal disaggregation considered. This implies that the closer we look at the intra-urban structure, the more likely we are to perceive it as an unstable system.

The analysis now shifts to the case of relative growth. Due to the fact that there are three different ways to constrain the relative growth version of the model (depending upon the particular type of formation available), there are three different stability conditions one can obtain.

As the system is conservative in parts, the overall community inter-action matrix is not anti-symmetric, although parts of it are. The system is in a continuous disequilibrium. Particular properties among the original interaction coefficients must hold for each type of conservation condition used. Not all need be congruent. This leads to the conclusion that depending upon the observed qualitative properties of the dynamic equilibrium, one can obtain information as to the appropriate conservation condition to be used.

G. INTRA-URBAN PREDICTION, PARSIMONY, AND POLICY ANALYSIS

The discussion of the theoretical framework and its associated six particular phenomena of intra-urban dynamics relied exclusively on qualitative observations regarding these events as they manifested themselves in zones of US metropolitan areas during the past thirty years or so. Prediction of these events for zones not having already experienced them requires additional analysis. Accessibility seems to be a variable along which one could identify possible candidates for such events among the zones of a SMSA. Topography and other locational endowments also play a role in such predictions.

However, the most important determinant for identifying urban locations' (zones) candidates for these cycles seems to be relative age of the built capital stock in the zone and, its related variable, average rela-tive quality level. Accessibility is related to age, as districts developed in more recent time-periods seem also to have experienced increases in relative accessibility to other zones in the urban space, whereas older zones seems to have experienced declines in their relative accessibility. A theory of intra-urban forecasting still awaits rigorous empirical research so that the relevant variables can be identified along which one can determine candidacy of a zone for these events to occur. Above all, consistent time-series data are needed.

Declines in relative transportation costs following heavy transpor-tation investment levels were a factor in suburbanization and neigh-bourhood tipping in the US. Increases in relative transportation costs (including energy costs and congestion) were factors behind centraliz-ation and gentrification. Another host of factors has been identified in the urban literature as having contributed to these and other events. Changes in preferences, rises in income, local fiscal conditions, taxation policies from a national standpoint, and technological innovations, are notable examples. The analysis presented here is capable of generating these events, however, without resorting to a large number of variables; instead, it reproduces the main qualitative features of past behaviour using a minimum number of variables and parameters. It also reproduces a limited number of events that could possibly be experienced by various land uses and/or zones. Although one cannot precisely predict what will happen to a land use or a zone, one obtains through this analysis a small number of alternative futures. These futures apparently fall under a very limited inter-zonal and inter-use association, namely, the predatory kind. More will be added on this in Part IV.

In the framework of the dynamic ecological analysis public policy intervention must be construed as perturbation of dynamical paths either at the inter- or intra-urban level. The result of such perturbations might be a shift to a neighbouring path of a developmental motion; or it could be a shift in a parameter value identifying a particular ecology type defining the developmental path. The latter could result in either a neighbouring steady state with the same dynamical properties at equilibrium as the one disturbed, or in a transition from one ecology to another, thus effecting evolutionary change through shifts in the nature of the dynamical equilibria. Environmental perturbation or public policy, finally, could result in changes in parameter values at critical levels, which do not necessarily identify a switch to a different ecology (the a^0 and b^0 of intra-urban dynamics discussed earlier). These perturbations, none the less, may result in evolutionary change as critical thresholds within the various intra-urban ecologies are approached.

What then must be investigated is the properties of the area of the landscape over which developmental change can be absorbed without undesirable evolutionary transition; the location of the initial perturbation in the landscape and its neighbourhood; and finally the magnitude of the policy intervention, relative to the dynamic stability domain prevailing in the particular locale of the landscape. A precise mapping of a metropolitan section of the intra-urban landscape will have to await the extensive data collection and analysis alluded to earlier. As census data accumulate over time, the efforts for testing along these lines will become more meaningful.

Very often, the inability of planning to effect change of an evolutionary or developmental type has been attributed to failures of planning. However, one element is often missing from that discussion, which is critical: a proper study of the part of the landscape over which the implementing force is applied and the relative magnitude of the intervention. Addressing questions such as these may be fruitful in obtaining insights into the effectiveness or desirability of specific intra-urban public actions.

H. STOCHASTICITY AND DETERMINISM IN INTRA-URBAN DYNAMICS

The scale of analysis in dealing with intra-urban dynamics issues is drastically reduced from that encountered at the inter-urban level. As one moves to lower scales, the possibility that micro-behaviour will affect to a significant extent macro-behaviour becomes stronger. This section thus sets the stage for examining the possibility that at the intra-urban level micro-behaviour shapes macro-performance. In doing so, a macro-density-dependent micro-behaviour formulation of locational decision is proposed. Stochasticity in behaviour is incorporated.

By making appropriate assumptions regarding disaggregated (individual) behaviour, and aggregation of disaggregated actions, the aggregate behaviour of zonal rent–density interactions is examined. The results of such assumptions are then empirically tested. The driving question is whether a deterministic (mean value) equation of aggregate behaviour is replicating well enough observed dynamics in zonal density–rent interactions. This mean value equation is the aggregation of individual behaviour from the stochastic master equation so that particular assumptions regarding non-linearity are met. Specifically, the assumptions call for the stochastic master equation to have a single hump.

It is concluded that (i) a deterministic mean value equation is quite adequate in depicting aggregate zonal density–rent interactions; (ii) individual behaviour is sufficiently uniform so that an approximation to a simple typical agent is adequate; and (iii) the deterministic mean value models for intra-urban dynamics are useful descriptors of intra-urban phenomena. The first finding has significant epistemological implications for intra-urban dynamics in particular and urban evolution in general. These implications will be more closely analysed in Part IV and the Epilogue. Here, the formulation of the land use density–rent interactions will be provided in Section H.1; in Section H.2 the stochastic master equation formulation will be given; and in Section H.3 the empirical evidence will be presented.

1. Land rent, density, and oscillatory dynamics in land use

The purpose of this brief section is to provide the basic deterministic model of cyclical behaviour in land values (rent) and land use density of capital improvement at particular zones in the urban space. Urban land is viewed here as a commodity over which speculative development and transactions occur, on the basis of future expected utilization levels. Shocks, in the form of sudden changes in parameters exogenous to the particular zone and due to an area-wide change of circumstances, do take place and affect speculation. Such shocks, however, will be assumed not to occur for the purpose of this exposition. Also, fluctuations in behaviour due to agents' differences exist. At the end of this section it will be shown how the deterministic equations model can be transformed into a stochastic master equation, so that individual differences in the form of fluctuations in the agents' behaviour at the aggregate level can be accommodated.

Assume a relatively small zone within a large metropolitan area. Let x_0 be the number of individuals that belong to a specific land use activity allocated at this particular zone at time-period t_0. For example, this particular activity could be the number of families of a 'four-member household in a single-family detached unit, on a quarter-acre lot, owner-occupied dwelling' residential type. At this intial time-period t_0 the suppliers of the land improvement quote an asking price of $r_0(t_0)$.

The initial asking price is derived on the basis of expectations that in the long run $\bar{x}$ individuals of this particular activity will be located in that zone, and that the suppliers did supply housing enough to accommodate $\bar{x}$. Thus, $r_0(t_0)$ is the uniform rental series over a time-horizon which maximizes the discounted suppliers' expected profit. According to this formulation the suppliers have foresight and expectations for the steady state, but not for the dynamics toward the steady state. On the demand side, the $x_0(t_0)$ is in response to the willingness to pay (bid price) per unit area of land, per capita, at that particular zone at the steady state. This bid-rent $\bar{r}$ is estimated on the basis of a density level $\bar{x}$. This bid price $\bar{r}$ is not known to the suppliers with certainty, and in general the asking price $r_0(t_0)$ will be different from $\bar{r}$. Thus, the demand sector has expectations for $\bar{x}$ at the steady state, but not for the intermediate dynamics. At any time-period t they are faced simply with an asking price $r(t)$.

Assume now that deterministic dynamic adjustments in x and r take place simultaneously. These adjustments depend upon the differences between the long-term anticipations and the current levels according to the following dynamics

$$\dot{x} = \alpha(\bar{r} - r)x$$
$$\dot{r} = \gamma(x - \bar{x})r.$$

If the current suppliers' asking price r drops below the agents' willingness to pay $\bar{r}$ then more individuals in this activity will move into the zone increasing its density x, whereas the density will drop if the bid price is below the asking price. On the supply side, if the current occupancy level is below the speculated $\bar{x}$ for suppliers, they will be motivated to decrease the asking rent, whereas if it is above the anticipated density level $\bar{x}$ they will be motivated to increase the current asking land price. This is a simple demand–supply model of speculative land rent under foresight with partially congruent expectations from demanders and suppliers. It is consistent with transactions in commodities in futures markets. It is also equivalent to the general Volterra–Lotka system, producing neutral stability with clockwise motion in the (x, r) space (Fig. III.7 (a)).

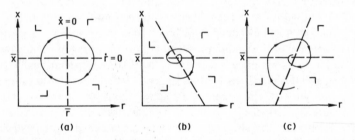

FIG. III.7. *The rent (r)-land use density (x) deterministic interaction* (a) absence of density externality results in neutral stability; (b) under negative external effects, due to density, the land use accumulation process becomes a source; (c) under positive external effects, intra-group attraction, the process results in a sink

Assume now that density is an externality, negatively affecting the particular land use activity agglomeration in a zone. Then this effect can be depicted by

$$\dot{x} = \alpha(\bar{r} - r)x - \beta x^2$$

where β is positive. The end-result is a source spiral out of the neighbourhood with oscillatory motion in both rental and activity levels. The neighbourhood density–rent interactions produce an unstable oscillatory motion resulting in ever-increasing fluctuations in rental and density patterns (Fig. III.7 (b)). If, on the other hand, the effect of density is positive, $\beta < 0$ (a condition associated with intra-group attraction), then the result is a sink with spiralling motion (Fig. III.7 (c)). At $\beta = 0$ the bifurcation point is located so that at its vicinity sources are turned into sinks through centres as β decreases. The motion remains oscillatory (Fig. III.7 (c)).

Parameter β's composition can be viewed as the net difference of negative and positive forces in depicting intra-group attraction. If the externalities of agglomeration outweigh the intra-group sympathy then the value of β is negative. However, β's magnitude also depends upon monopoly/monopsony conditions for that particular activity at that particular zone in the urban area. Zoning policies may be viewed as constraints in the (r, x) space either as rent controls, or as maximum density constraints, or both. These exogenous frontiers in the (r, x) space may result in additional (border) equilibria. The above deterministic set of simultaneous differential equations which provide the simultaneous motion in rental and density levels can now be made stochastic.

One is motivated in reformulating the above problem in a stochastic fashion for a number of reasons. First, by formulating the problem in a master equation fashion one can depict the micro-foundations of macro-behaviour. Second, by possibly arriving at the mean value deterministic equation of the stochastic master equation, one can identify the differences between modelling directly macro-behaviour versus modelling macro-behaviour through some aggregation procedure of micro-behaviour. The differences in the dynamic equilibria and possible bifurcation in behaviour under the two modes of approaching macro-behaviour will make more explicit the criteria under which one method is more appropriate than the other. A general formulation will be supplied first, and then a specific model will be discussed.

2. The stochastic master equation for rent–density interactions

Assume that x is the portion of the agents in that particular activity that decide to locate in the zone under examination, so that $1 - x$ locate in the balance of the urban area. Each agent in this population has a probability of entering or leaving the zone or the rest of the city, at time t. The probability $p_{x\uparrow}$ of entering the zone is equal to the probability of leaving the area designated as the balance of the city, $q_{x\downarrow}$. Similarly, the probability of leaving the zone $p_{x\downarrow}$ is equal to $q_{x\uparrow}$. Assume that these transition probabilities define a Markov process of agents' distribution in the zone and the rest of the city. Then the dynamics of observing a particular population distribution P_x is

$$\frac{dP_x}{dt} = x\left[p_{x\uparrow} P_x - p_{x\downarrow}(1 - P_x)\right].$$

This is a macro-level stochastic master equation which accounts for fluctuations due to individual behaviour at the micro-level. Probability $P_{x\uparrow}$ is a function of the macro-level specification of the system (the x, r and $\bar{x}$, $\bar{r}$) and could follow Volterra–Lotka dynamics or any other aggregate density-dependent individual dynamic behaviour theoretical construct. The probability P_x of observing the system population distribution x at time-period t could be such that it is distributed around some mean value $\bar{x}$ (although it could have more than one peak).

This is an interesting formulation, because it produces macro-behaviour in two steps: first, when the density-dependent behaviour of individual action was stated, the *macro-foundations of micro-behaviour were set*. Then the uniformity in behaviour assumption and the subsequent aggregation of individual actions produces the *micro-foundations of macro-behaviour*. One could also state a stochastic equation describing aggregate behaviour dynamics based on typical individual action. Although this is not done here, it would constitute the micro-foundations of macro-behaviour without involving aggregation directly. The analysis returns now to the originally stated problem.

On the supply side, if there is no collusion among the various sellers of capital improvement in the zone, which could result in a uniform rent being quoted as the asking price, one might assume that a probability distribution exists for the rents charged inside the zone. After an initial perturbation $r_0(t_0)$ arrived at through suppliers' expectations on some long-term land use pattern, there are increases and declines in $r(t)$ based on current conditions, as outlined earlier. However, here each supplier has a transition probability of accumulating or depleting r, $p_{r\uparrow}$, or $p_{r\downarrow}$, from one level to a neighbouring one. It is assumed, following standard master equation formalization (Nicolis and Prigogine, 1977, p. 231) that these transition probabilities follow a Markov process so that at each stage a Volterra–Lotka dynamic identifies the relevant kinetics. Assume now that a probability, P_r, exists of observing a particular rent distribution $\bar{r}$. The mean value vector $\bar{r}$ contains the rent asked inside the zone and the opportunity cost in terms of rental price for the population in this category of land use for the rest of the town. The stochastic master equation for the rent side of the density–price intra-urban interactions is

$$\frac{dP_r}{dt} = r[p_{r\uparrow} P_r - p_{r\downarrow} (1 - P_r)].$$

In the case where P is highly concentrated around the mean values $\tilde{x}$ and $\tilde{r}$, then the above two stochastic master equations dP_x/dt, dP_r/dt become the following approximate mean values simultaneous ordinary differential equations

$$\frac{d\tilde{x}}{dt} = \tilde{x}[p_{x\uparrow} \tilde{x} - p_{x\downarrow} (1 - \tilde{x})]$$

$$\frac{d\tilde{r}}{dt} = \tilde{r}[p_{r\uparrow} \tilde{r} - p_{r\downarrow} (1 - \tilde{r})].$$

W. Weidlich and G. Haag (1980, 1983) have shown that these mean values equations, under exponential, density-dependent micro-behaviour specifications, could result in a multiplicity of phase diagrams. A Volterra–Lotka specification for P_x and P_r reproduces through mean value equations a phase portrait equivalent to the deterministic ones, as Haag and Dendrinos (1983) have demonstrated (Appendix IX). This is a very important finding. It makes clear that under well-accepted economic assumptions, the stochastic master equation provides qualitatively equivalent results to the deterministic mean value equation. What is needed then, is to test this deterministic mean value equation empirically. If it holds, then the key assumptions made here hold. It would also demonstrate that for the purpose of examining aggregate behaviour it is not necessary explicitly to account for individual behaviour.

3. Empirical testing of the land use density–rent model

The results presented here draw from the work by Dendrinos and Haag (1984). Time-series data from twelve US SMSAs were used for the 1950–80 period. These SMSAs are listed in Appendix IX. Aggregate data on population density and average rent per unit area of land were employed, at the central cities and suburb levels of metropolitan areas. Use of intra-urban population migration counts was made. For reasons of data limitations, it was necessary to assume that a number of the model's parameters do not vary from one metropolitan area to another, and that all remain constant over time (see Appendix IX).

It was conclusively shown that a deterministic set of mean value equations on relative density and rental value is a very good descriptor of their interaction in a sample of US metropolitan areas. Further, evidence was supplied to show that a cyclical pattern (of spiralling sink type) is the underlying kinetic. Tables III.2, 3, 4 present the simulated and actual counts for the Portland (Oregon), San Diego (California), and Philadelphia (Pennsylvania) SMSAs for the rent–density interactions during the period 1950–80 and the forecast for 1990.

In Fig. III.8 the phase portrait of the dynamic equilibrium in rent–density interactions derived from a sample of twelve US SMSAs is shown. It is a spiralling sink identifying a stable attractor where the

TABLE III.2. *Actual and simulated counts of Portland, Oregon SMSA; central city–suburban ring rent–density interactions: 1950–90*

Year	x		y	
	Simulated	Actual	Simulated	Actual
1950	−.068	−.068	.979	.979
1960	−.275	−.234	.961	.966
1970	−.441	−.381	.938	.944
1973	−.482	−.438	.929	NA
1975	−.507	−.491	.924	NA
1976	−.518	−.457	.921	NA
1977	−.530	−.465	.918	NA
1978	−.540	−.510	.915	NA
1980	−.561	−.553	.909	.908
1990	−.639		.876	

TABLE III.3. *San Diego, California SMSA; rent-density interactions: 1950–90*

Year	x		y	
	Simulated	Actual	Simulated	Actual
1950	.022	.022	.988	.988
1960	−.283	−.343	.972	.967
1970	−.508	−.526	.948	.942
1973	−.558	−.551	.939	NA
1975	−.586	−.584	.933	NA
1976	−.599	−.594	.930	NA
1977	−.612	−.607	.927	NA
1978	−.623	−.621	.924	NA
1980	−.644	−.644	.917	.921
1990	−.712		.883	

TABLE III.4. *Philadelphia, Pennsylvania SMSA; rent-density interactions 1950-90*

Year	x		y	
	Simulated	Actual	Simulated	Actual
1950	.129	.129	.944	.944
1960	−.025	−.077	.918	.913
1970	−.160	−.190	.885	.870
1973	−.197	−.225	.874	NA
1975	−.221	−.244	.866	NA
1976	−.232	−.251	.862	NA
1977	−.244	−.258	.858	NA
1978	−.254	−.264	.854	NA
1980	−.276	−.279	.845	.841
1990	−.369		.800	

suburban share of population and land rent value exceeds that of the central cities of metropolitan areas. The simulation runs indicate that although during the calibration period (1950-80) no oscillation is present by the year 1990 the population shift to the suburbs is expected to be reversed. Surburbs will continue to enlarge their share of land value (in Fig. III.8 a movement from north to south implies an increase

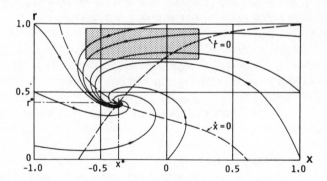

FIG. III.8. *The phase portrait of the land use mean value density–rent dynamic equilibrium for twelve US metropolitan areas.*
Variables *x* (land use) and *r* (density) are normalized so that they vary between − 1 and + 1. The shaded area shows the location of the recorded paths for the twelve SMSAs studied

in rental value share for the suburbs, whereas a movement from east to west is associated with an increase in the suburbs' population share).

Although the analysis indicated that regional location and age do not play a major role for location in the phase portrait, size of metropolitan area does affect their place in the phase portrait: the larger the size, the closer towards the steady state is the dynamic path. This and other related conclusions are further discussed in Dendrinos and Haag (1984).

I. CONCLUSIONS

Internal urban dynamics were reviewed in an intra-zonal as well as inter-zonal urban ecological framework. Intra-zonal urban ecology consists of inter-land use competition for space; whereas inter-zonal ecology is comprised of competition among various zones for a particular land use.

Contrary to inter-urban dynamics, extensively disaggregated internal urban dynamics are expected to be unstable. Although the selective group of intra-urban phenomena analysed was found to belong to predator–prey ecology, the particular class of predatory Volterra–Lotka dynamics found to be pertinent descriptors of intra-urban ecology result in exclusion, i.e. one of the two relevant species becoming extinct.

Six particular internal urban phenomena were examined: neighbourhood tipping and gentrification; suburbanization and centralization; slum formation and preservation. These events were viewed in the framework of bifurcating behaviour in ecological dynamics. Each pair of events was found to be the outcome of a reversed motion towards an equilibrium associated with competitive exclusion. In each of the three cases, a change in the nature of the dynamic equilibrium associated with exclusion produced a switch from one event (for example, suburbanization) to the other (centralization). Consequently, the six events are classified as belonging to three groups of urban ecological phenomena characterized by evolutionary change. The broad class of ecological problems describing these events belongs to predator–prey dynamics.

Instability in internal urban dynamics was attributed to locational proximity. This must result in a highly interconnected (or quite close to random) community matrix and very likely identifying unstable interactions. Evidence of explosive growth and extinction among various land uses in intra-urban dynamics is abundant in metropolitan areas of the US. It supports the hypothesis of random interconnectance.

At a more aggregative level, the topic of micro-foundations of macro-behaviour in intra-urban dynamics was also analysed within the framework of a land use density and rent dynamic model. At first, the macro-foundation of micro-behaviour was identified as a density-(macro) dependent probabilistic individual (micro) behaviour. Then, in a stochastic framework, the micro-foundations of macro-behaviour were laid out; through aggregation of individual behaviour, the stochastic macro-behaviour was identified.

Under particular assumptions regarding uniformity of behaviour at the micro-level (namely that the stochastic master equation has one hump) mean value (deterministic) equations were derived for macro-(system) behaviour. It was found that indeed such assumptions do hold for the case of land use density–rent interactions. In view of the fundamental nature of this location-allocation problem (being at the heart of intra-urban dynamics) it was concluded that it is proper to model internal urban dynamics in a deterministic mode, at an appropriate level of aggregation.

The problem of land use density–rent interaction was analysed in detail. First, the deterministic aggregate density–rent model was presented in a Volterra–Lotka predator–prey-type ecological framework; conditions for stability were shown, and the oscillatory nature of the interaction was identified. Next, the stochastic formulation of the problem was supplied, where the use of the stochastic master equation formulation was shown. Using empirical evidence from a number of US SMSAs at the central city–suburb level the two-zone residential density–rent interaction model was tested, and the results were presented. It was demonstrated that the interaction is a stable spiralling sink type dynamic in the relative density–rent space.

The implications of these results will be further explored in the next Part (section F), where aspects of determinism and stochasticity in urban evolution will be investigated.

Part IV.

EPISTEMOLOGICAL ASPECTS OF URBAN EVOLUTION

A. INTRODUCTION: THE PROCESS OF SELECTION

Selection in the field of urban ecology refers to the choice of a particular set of values (and signs) of the coefficients in the community matrix. Each set of values depicts the selection of a type of interaction among interconnected populations. As these values change so does the interconnectance type. Changes in population levels for the interacting systems towards their steady state, given fixed values of the community matrix coefficients, are fast movements. Changes in the values of the community matrix coefficients constitute slow movements, i.e. movement to a new selection set.

Evolution is associated with change in the nature of the fast motion involved in a community of interacting populations, due to selection passing through some critical thresholds in its slow motion. Selection occurs continuously in the space of real values of the community matrix coefficients. However, as selection spans this space, it does not always result in evolutionary events. Developmental paths, namely dynamic paths towards a steady state, are perturbed. At times the steady state is shocked. The nature of the dynamic path remains unaffected as smooth slow motions occur in most of the paramater space.

The following is a discussion drawn from the richness of the Darwinian paradigm; it lays out the basic notions of an epistemology of urban evolution based on selection and associated concepts. In section B, the topic of selection is defined in urban interacting systems. Then in section C the notion of selection is approached from the viewpoint of an optimization process; there the notions of environmental adjustment and adaptation by urban systems are presented. In section D, aspects of stability and selection are addressed in the inter- and intra-urban contexts. After a brief look at urban innovation (introduction of new towns, land uses, zones, and their effects on stability), aspects of determinism, chance, and prediction in urban theory and modelling are discussed in section E.

B. SELECTION IN URBAN ECOLOGY

In this section two particular topics of selection are addressed; first, the question whether the selection process favours at different time-periods particular urban settings at the inter-urban level and specific activities zones in the intra-urban context, or whole communities of interacting urban systems. Second, selection variability in urban ecology is examined drawing from the empirical evidence presented. Certain conclusions regarding habitual behaviour by urban systems are reached.

1. Survival of urban communities

A number of ecologists, for example Smith (1974), argue that the selection process favours the survival of particular individuals (or groups) within a species by promoting and sustaining characteristics which ensure their perpetuation within a particular environment at specific time-periods. It does not make sense to assume otherwise; ecologists argue that it is not reasonable to expect natural selection to act upon ecosystems as a whole, or favour stability properties of communities of interacting species in particular.

Smith identifies two ways that selection at the species level can produce stability. He calls these two processes 'coevolution through genetic feedback' and 'species exclusion'. In the first process, the interaction of two species is viewed as affecting genetic changes in either or both of the species because of their interaction. Changes may be such for each species that stable interconnectance is established and maintained. In the second case, island communities can exist because they have selectively accepted from a pool of immigrating species those that provide stable (and beneficial to all coexisting species) interconnectance.

For urban analysts this is a point of departure from general ecology. Contrary to plant and non-human animal communities, in urban ecology the selection process favours not only individual populations but whole communities as well. Urban systems are, after all, governed by a large number of units of government at various levels. Such governance might be weak or strong, its functions may be explicit or implicit. But governance exists none the less.

Alongside individual decentralized decision-making by consumers, firms, and local or special purpose governments (all of which express their own interests as well as, under altruistic behaviour, the interests of others), there are also collective, centrally derived decisions implemented by higher or general purpose governments. Governments represent aggregations of individual choices, expressed through a social choice rule.

In a soup of decision-making from all these agents aggregate social selection occurs. This selection, either at the inter-urban or the intra-urban contexts, can be construed as associated with a particular set of coefficients in the relative urban interaction matrix. As a result of this selection, fast dynamics take place. As long as the system does not further act to change these dynamics, the system can be considered as having selected them; this selection may not have been explicitly made, but this system has adopted it by not reacting to it. As a result cities grow and decline, neighbourhoods (zones) and/or land uses rise and fall. These dynamic patterns have been shaped, at any time-period, by the collective effect of all individual actions. The end-result of such collective (cumulative) effects is the magnitude and sign of the urban community matrix coefficients.

This soup of decentralized and centrally derived decisions produces a selection of coefficients in the urban community matrix resulting in an aggregate regularity at both the inter- and intra-urban level. Based on evidence presented in this book, the population levels of the interacting groups are shown to obey predator-prey Volterra–Lotka dynamics. The selection process in urban ecology is found to favour a particular community (as opposed to one-factor) dynamic, through a multiplicity of decision-making apparatuses. However, the urban system as a whole reacts to these individual fast dynamics. There is a feedback between these dynamics and the coefficients of the community matrix. As a result, the coefficients do not remain constant over extended time-horizons. There is a slow motion in the system that modifies them as the outcome of collective selection. In the intra-urban level the selection process is shown to result in the phenomena of suburbanization, slum formation, gentrification, at certain instances. Analysis of the qualitative properties of these events demonstrated that evolutionary change emerged from collective urban selection during the past thirty years. This evolutionary change emerged as collective urban selection smoothly varied certain key interaction parameters, at specific points, so that these smooth changes resulted in drastic modification of the behaviour of the urban system.

In summary: the selection process in urban ecology favours whole community dynamics rather than individual group development. This is due to the collective decision-making of public agencies and individuals.

Evolutionary change has been at times the result of urban selection at the intra-urban level.

2. *Selection in the urban landscape*

Empirical investigation indicates that the selection process exhibits a rather limited range of behaviour. Table II.2 shows that in inter-urban dynamics parameter space, comprising the speeds of relative income and population adjustments as well as the relative population friction coefficient in the inter-urban Volterra–Lotka formalism, selection occupies a very small window in the landscape. This finding lends support to the proposition that selection in inter-urban dynamics seems to be highly restrictive.

One can hypothesize that an urban ecological habit must be in operation, which strongly affects urban systems behaviour. If selection is viewed as the outcome of an optimizing process, then the topography of the optimization surface must be very steep at this locale. A very strong attractor must be present locally.

C. SELECTION AS AN OPTIMIZATION PROCESS: ENVIRONMENTAL ADJUSTMENT AND ADAPTATION

Selection, in human (and urban) behaviour, implies some form of optimization process at work. Any optimization process consists of the following elements: objective function(s); a set of pertinent constraints defining the feasibility set; and an algorithm of search towards the optimum. This algorithm identifies a choice rule for selecting alternative points in the feasibility set; an evaluation rule for estimating the value of the objective function for each alternative selected; and a stopping rule for terminating the search once an optimum (local or global) point has been found.

It is not clear what that selection entails for the field of general mathematical ecology, in terms of objective function(s), constraints, and selection algorithm. For example: is there an objective function together with a set of constraints and a selection algorithm present in the environment of a given species or community of species? How does this manifest itself? It is reasonable to assume that objective functions, constraints, and selection algorithms are present in the behaviour of each species; are they identical for all members of each species? Emlen (1973) examines fitness of species as an environmental adaptation process, methodologically very similar to the neo-classical micro-economic theory of consumption and production. Fitness levels are viewed equivalently to utility and profit functions. Curry (1981) uses this method in a labour market context for various occupations.

A basic ingredient of optimization theory is that there are many possible selection algorithms for a given optimization problem. Some are more efficient in finding the optimum than others. Biologists in general do not view natural selection as the result of an optimization process, chiefly because one cannot answer how the selection among alternative selection algorithms is carried out for each species, whether these two selection processes are carried out simultaneously or sequentially, and how this selection process is coded and replicated. Population genetics could provide some of these answers but has not done so yet. In mathematical ecology, all aspects of behaviour are assumed to be coded in the Volterra-Lotka formalism and the community matrix. Thus, the coefficients of this matrix contain the required information effectively simulating the behaviour of interacting species within a specified environment, without the need to resort to an optimizing process.

Some informative points can be made by looking at urban ecology along lines of optimization. Individual agents, consumers, firms, and governments operate under a multiplicity of objective functions: individual utility and profit functions for consumers and producers; social welfare functions used by governments. They also operate under a multiplicity of perceived resource constraints, a variety of budgets and expectations. Governments in particular operate under explicit or implicit aggregate social objective functions of various kinds and subject to economic, political, and social constraints. All these units carry different search algorithms.

As in the case of general ecology, one can assume that all that information is coded in the coefficients of the interaction matrix in a particular community of urban groups within a particular environment. In plant and non-human animal ecology, within each species, the typical member's behaviour might be highly skewed towards a mean value: for humans, it may be rather flat, or with multiple humps. This, it could be argued, is a major difference between general ecology and urban ecology. In the light of this possibility, the empirical evidence and resulting implications and use of a stochastic master equation formulation of non-linear urban dynamic behaviour becomes informative.

As discussed in Part III, H, regarding land use density and rent interaction, at the central city–suburb scale there seems to be an acceptable degree of uniformity in intra-urban behaviour. It allows for the use of deterministic aggregate mean value equations effectively to simulate seemingly stochastic micro-derived aggregate behaviour. Thus, it appears safe to assume that in urban systems of the scale studied in this book, all the complexity of individual behaviour is coded in the aggregate interaction matrix. For the purpose of modelling the system's aggregate behaviour, one can do as well by simulating directly the aggregate behaviour of the urban systems rather than by some aggregation of (seemingly quite similar) disaggregative behaviour.

Adopting a perspective according to which the cumulative effects of disaggregated behaviour are depicted in the selection of a particular set of group interaction coefficients begs the question: What exactly is coded in these coefficients for a selection to be made? In order to answer this question, one must take a broader view involving an optimization process.

Although nobody has yet derived it, there can be stated a least-effort integral whose first-order minimization conditions provide a set of equations from which the Volterra-Lotka fast dynamics, for a particular community of interacting groups, could be obtained. This, in the general case, is not a potential, as it is in Volterra's conservative systems. The corresponding integrand can be viewed as a *least-effort adjustment function* of a particular community of groups (urban subsystems) to the given environment. The information of the environment and the group's reaction to it are coded in the dynamics associated with the coefficients of the urban community matrix. They result in a *fast* movement by the interacting groups toward a steady state. The selection processes, collectively, are embedded in the dynamics of the community matrix.

A second integral can be further stated (yet to be derived, too) which can provide as its first-order condition a set of equations from which the particular set of the community matrix coefficients can be obtained. Its integrand must be viewed as a *least-effort adaptation function* of a particular community of groups (urban subsystems) to the given environment. Again, the information of the environment and the community's reaction to it are coded in the dynamics of change in the coefficients of the community matrix. This selection constitutes a *slow* movement. The fast movement is nested in the least-effort adjustment function covering relatively short time-spans. Its effect is continuous over extended time-horizons. On the other hand the slow movement is nested in the least-effort adaptation function. Whether slow motion is continuous or discontinuous is still an open question. Empirical evidence from aggregate urban dynamics (the Miami and Seattle SMSAs) points to a discontinuous movement lasting relatively short time-periods. Thus, one might speculate that slow movements may be nested in spurts occurring discontinuously over extended time-horizons. Further, the manner by which urban subsystems react to an environment, and the way the environment reacts to these urban units can be considered as contained in a single integrand with two time-scales involving a longer-term adaptation and a shorter-term adjustment process. This, two time-scales integrand, is the carrier of the collective selection process.

In interpreting this least-effort integral and its algorithm for search of an optimum, one might attribute its existence and form to the collective memory, norms, and actions not of a single individual agent, but the community as a whole. Social, economic, and political institutions carry and transmit the code which results in development, evolution, and adaptation of interacting groups. Selection, as suggested here, occurs simultaneously at various levels. A number of ways have been proposed recently to simulate the decision-making soup of the various agents of an urban and regional system. Cruz (1980) suggests, along the lines of Nash equilibrium strategies in differential game theory, a leader–follower (fast–slow) system of differential equations. Fisk and Boyce (1983) propose a generalized non-linear complementarity problem of agent decision-making, where the first-order conditions are Kuhn-Tucker conditions of a system-wide non-linear optimality problem. Parenthetically, their first-order conditions are identical to the isoclines of a generalized Volterra–Lotka system.

In summary, in the field of urban ecology selection implies some optimization process at work. This optimization process results in selection of particular group associations and group dynamics. The collective effects of all groups' behaviour are embedded in the community interaction coefficients. Further, through the governing of a stipulated potential depicting collective least-effort adjustment and adaptation functions, fast and slow urban dynamics occur. They result in abrupt evolutionary change in the urban systems behaviour at certain time-periods when critical points in the urban landscapes are approached.

D. SELECTION, COMPLEXITY, AND STABILITY

A key factor in the evolution of the urban systems is that of stability. Whether or not selection favours stability within a set of urban settings at the inter-urban level, or a set of neighbourhoods or land uses at the intra-urban level can be detected from empirical evidence. Available information covering the past century or so, where time-series have been collected on selected variables recording urban growth/decline patterns, seems to suggest that selection has favoured stability in inter-urban dynamics and instability in intra-urban interactions at a very disaggregative level.

A very large number of cities comprise the urban sector of the US. The relative growth in all cities surveyed points towards stable dynamic behaviour, as no cities were found to grow continuously over the past ninety years, and no metropolitan area has been or is currently driven to extinction within this time-span. It must be thus concluded that the urban sector of the US must not be randomly interconnected within this time-span. The cities of the US must be interacting in a highly non-random fashion.

The very large number of land uses within cities, the variety of districts comprising a large urban area, and their relative locational proximity — all these characteristics present the prerequisite conditions for unstable intra-urban dynamics. This leaves small towns, or cities with a highly selective, non-random interconnectance to exhibit an internally stable dynamic structure. It is likely that these might be pathological cases depicting stagnating towns or towns which are rigidly planned.

Space and its particular manifestation as distance separating cities at the inter-urban level and zones or land uses at the intra-urban level must operate differently in these two cases. Clearly, it is a factor in both levels of interacting units. However, its importance must not be the same. Overcoming impedance could be one of the key elements in the selection process determining the magnitude of interaction at the intra-urban level. However, other factors seem to play the key role in the highly selective interaction process underlying inter-urban dynamics.

Net expected gains (or pay-offs) obtained at the origin and destination of a particular interacting pair must be the determinant of the magnitude and sign of interaction. These net gains, viewed in a relative framework, identify comparative advantages present in a particular interaction. A non-random distribution of comparative advantages must imply a non-random interconnectance pattern. At the intra-urban level distance seems to shape the relative distribution of such advantages through accessibility differentials. Such differentials give place to factors affecting export-oriented industrial activity location. These factors may have less to do with pure access differentials and more with an uneven distribution of natural resources and topographical features. In this case, the particular topographical structure and initial distribution of natural resources within a national economy may dictate the properties of stability or instability of its urban sector.

Another factor, possibly contributing to stability in inter-urban spatial interaction, could be lack of perfect information for economic agents (producers, consumers, and governments). As it is not economically feasible to obtain perfect information regarding all possible spatial interaction net pay-offs, this must produce selective behaviour regarding interconnectance. Erroneous or collusive expectations could be another cause for highly selective inter-urban interaction patterns. Uneven distribution of risks in locational decisions is yet another. The effect of the latter factors must drastically diminish in intra-urban dynamics, where the importance of distance is radically increased.

E. SELECTION AND INNOVATION IN URBAN EVOLUTION

Two issues will be briefly addressed in this section where questions will be mostly raised rather than answers provided: the question of what happens to stability in case of new entry conditions in urban systems, and whether selection favours stability by stifling innovation in urban ecology. Adopting the perspective that collective selection is embedded in the coefficients of the urban community matrix has implications regarding the notion of innovation. These coefficients depict the game to be played and its rules, both in the long-term adaptation and the short-term adjustment phases. All actors' actions are presumably discounted in the selection process of these deterministic fast and slow dynamics.

Innovation implies the introduction of a new game: new rules and/or new players. New cities may enter the community of interacting urban areas in inter-urban dynamics. New land uses or new districts may be added to the interconnected community of uses and/or zones in intra-urban dynamics. New policies may enter the picture from the point of view of governments. These innovations may be induced from the environment as it changes. They may also be endogenously selected, embedded in the existing governing integrand: that information may be contained in the two time-scale optimizing function nesting an adjustment and adaptation process in a fixed environment. No new information may be required to depict this innovation; which one is true, one may never be able to answer: it is a metaphysical question. The formalism to state analytically the innovation problem is still to be developed. In case, one wishes to attempt it then one may ask: when does selection-induced innovation occur? Is it continuously present or does it operate in a discontinuous fashion? What triggers it? What is the mechanism for generating urban mutations?

From a policy standpoint, the issues are quite interesting. It is well accepted that policy development and evolution occur when policy voids are created (by mechanisms not yet known) and then selectively some policy voids are filled. What stimulates the genesis of policy voids (environmental changes or endogenous stimuli) is still widely debated in policy science.

Although one may not be able to answer directly such questions, one can say indirectly something regarding innovation and stability connections. New towns, new land uses, new districts, and new policies can enter stably or unstably interconnected urban systems. In stable interconnectance systems, which have not yet reached the May critical threshold level where instability can occur, new entries through migration can be accommodated without loss of stability properties. New towns can be added into the national space: as long as the critical value of interacting towns for the nation has not been exceeded, the nation's urban sector will continue to be stable. However, if the entry of a new town occurs when some critical value is near, in the number of towns existing in a nation with random strongly interconnected cities, then the new city may upset the stable properties of the urban sector. The new town may be itself driven to extinction, or it may force at least another town to extinction. It may produce explosive growth in some other city. Similar results are to be expected in the case of intra-urban land use. Entry of new populations into a town may or may not be destabilizing, and so may be new land uses.

Thus, in a highly interconnected environment where innovation is abundant, stability can be tested only when the environment is close enough to or has exceeded a critical threshold level regarding the number of interacting subsystems. In early stages of formation in a particular community of interacting urban systems, innovation is not destabilizing and can easily be accommodated. At later stages of development, however, when an environment has reached maturity in interaction among its subsystems, innovations might be detrimental to stability. Traditional (mature) environments may be able to withstand the shock of innovations, as long as they are either highly selective in their interconnectance or are able to extend their carrying capacity in terms of increasing the critical threshold's magnitude.

If selection (adaptation) favours stability, then it will result in supporting ample innovation or innovation diffusion in conditions far from the critical level when stability is disturbed. One might hypothesize that in mature environments, in communities close to their critical levels, selection might not favour stability by encouraging innovation. It might be that, through some higher-order optimizing function (least-effort integral) it could favour newer communities and the way to promote this is through the destabilization of older ones. This would necessitate the existence of some adaptation process expressing interests larger than that of the two communities. The fact that extinction of particular urban communities could be to the interest of the nation or some larger regions through the birth of new ones is only a case in point. The eventual decline of older communities within cities, cities within regions, regions within nations, and nations within a community of nations can be attributed to potentially such processes at work.

Selective transportation flows and trading patterns among towns, regions, and nations, as well as selective alliances among neighbourhoods, cities, regions, and nations can be justified on grounds of a selective process favouring stability. Innovation in such flows affecting interaction patterns may result in destabilization, locally or globally, of the community.

In summary, it is still an open question whether innovation implies introduction of new information into the interaction matrix (from the environment), or the governing optimizing function of adaptation contains such information. It is still, also, an open question whether selection favours innovation in stable urban systems, or in unstable ones.

F. URBAN DETERMINISM, NECESSITY, CHANCE, AND PREDICTION

Introduction of technological and policy innovations in urban dynamics can only be modelled as chance events due to lack of data. To accept, of course, a deterministic or a stochastic model in studying innovation implies the choice of a standpoint which cannot be currently defended, but only accepted *a priori*. Findings in the case of inter- and intra-urban dynamics seem to suggest that a deterministic view is sufficient to explain aggregate events lasting over a century of urban evolution. One need not resort to stochastic behaviour to replicate such events. The deterministic Volterra–Lotka formalism was identified as sufficient for replicating certain urban phenomena over a time-period of about 100 years. During this time-period small-scale slow dynamics were identified. However, their number was not high enough to depict statistically their driving forces. Common sense dictates that what is commonly perceived as technological or policy 'innovation' must have been abundant during this time-period. As a result one must have expected random walks in the dynamic paths of cities in the US. However, this did not occur. Deterministic models, at the inter-urban level and at a high level of aggregation at the intra-urban level, were found to be good descriptors of their dynamics.

It was not necessary to introduce exogenous innovation in the urban dynamic model studied, and stochastic modelling was not needed. This evidence seems to indicate that at this level of analysis a 'relative innovation' notion must be in operation. The relative innovation is sensitive only to these innovations that differentially affect various spatial systems. Such innovations must be rare and not result in a large-scale shock of the urban section of a nation.

All SMSAs were in existence during the time-horizon examined. Can one use such a deterministic framework to make predictions for the future? The answer depends on how much of an important role relative innovation plays in urban systems, on how one models innovation, and on how random relative innovation is (how much, where, and how new information is added to the model).

One may suppose that chance, at the level and scale of analysis presented, did not play a significant role in urban evolution in the US. Or, at least, one does not need to resort to outside (purely random) events to explain and replicate the patterns examined through quantitative empirical evidence. *Ex post facto*, one can account for all urban events (suburbanization, neighbourhood tipping, gentrification at the intra-urban level; spiralling sinks in relative aggregate growth at the inter-urban level) through the use of deterministic models of population dynamics; and by assuming very few changes in (a small number of) key parameters.

For urban systems chance may play a role over much longer time-spans than those studied here. Stochasticity may be important at even smaller scales of analysis than the intra-urban problems examined in this work. However, this may possibly be because of our lack of knowledge regarding the governing integral(s) in operation. In the selection process the mechanism for adaptation (i.e. the search algorithm for an either global or local optimum) the algorithm must leave a lot of room to chance. The search conditions are complex. There are many possible alternatives to be reached and evaluated in the least-effort adaptation process: they are characterized by highly non-linear interaction; there must be many local optima; there are many search procedures. All point towards a highly random process. In spite of all these, the urban environment seemingly behaves in a very particular way for relatively prolonged time-periods. It does not exhibit chaotic behaviour. It demonstrates reproducible patterns that exhibit very small variety. The process of selection in urban dynamics must be very informative.

Although regular patterns seem to occur in urban dynamics, the observed variety of performance is great enough, so that accurate prediction is not feasible to the degree one finds prediction possible in natural systems. In the case of inter-urban dynamics, the deterministic Volterra–Lotka formalism cannot really tell what will occur to any particular town in the US, which city will be perturbed in what parameters and by how much or when, or whether a city's carrying capacity will decrease drastically or increase dramatically after having been approached. The model can only tell what type of phenomena may occur, but cannot attribute these phenomena in the future to particular cities. Similarly, at the intra-urban case, the method can provide a classification of phenomena, but it cannot predict what zones will undergo gentrification, or at what precise time-period. Much more data are needed to attempt this, and even then there is no prior guarantee that such a bank will be able to supply accurate predictions. In urban systems prediction may not be possible, but chance (pure, that is) may have very little to do with it.

However, one ought to stress that whether or not predictions in urban systems turn out to be (or could be) accurate (or feasible at all) is of little importance. Of great interest, on the other hand, is the game-theoretic aspect of urban evolution: actors employ one another's expectations in order to form strategies of actions. Options markets, equivalent to the ones in operation in the stock exchange, however imperfect, also operate in urban systems: actors, act as if acquiring options contracts on various expectations. Urban actors incur bets on possible outcomes and as a result some activities end up dominating, whereas others become extinct. This line of approach to urban evolution seems to be insightful and fruitful to extend the present analysis. Lack of data, however, limits at present the modeller's capacity to simulate and test such games in futures markets.

EPILOGUE: SOME THOUGHTS ON THE INTERCONNECTANCE OF NATURAL AND URBAN SCIENCES AND THE MATHEMATICAL FORMALISM

Some thoughts, loosely connected at this stage, will be provided next regarding the nature of urban systems and their methodological equivalences to natural systems. One is impressed by the commonality in methods used and how the fields have evolved.

Urban systems operate in real time. Although limited experimentation does occur, one cannot repeat experiments as in chemistry, physics, or biology. Urban systems are historical and thus they are characterized by irreversibility. However, there is enough repetition in their behaviour, recorded over time, and there are enough regularities observed to allow for a theory of urban evolution to be constructed and selectively tested with empirical evidence.

Prediction, due to a variety of reasons, is not and cannot be very precise: multiplicity of equilibria, bifurcation, perturbations and randomness in individual behaviour and collective selection makes prediction into the future impossible at present. In spite of this, there is now the methodological framework for setting up alternative classes of phenomena as possible descriptors of selective, as currently expected, future urban events. The more aggregate the analysis and the closer the time-horizon, the more confidence one can have in these qualitative predictions. Empirical evidence seems to support this to an acceptable degree.

Although prediction cannot yet be asserted in the decisive manner found in natural sciences, understanding and knowledge of urban dynamical systems still can be obtained by using mathematical tools employed in the natural sciences, in particular, mathematical ecology. A dynamic theory of urban systems as presented here adheres to the dynamical theory of macro-biological systems and falls under the Darwinian epistemology. Urban systems are only a class of macro-biological systems and it is not surprising that direct methodological and empirical equivalences exist between the two.

Complexity and the micro-foundation of macro-behaviour are two topics which are common to both natural and urban science. It is now becoming apparent that the method to model these interactions in urban sciences is similar to the models used in the natural sciences. Two striking examples were presented in this book to make the point: the Volterra-Lotka formalism as describing macro-urban dynamic behaviour at the inter-urban level; and the master equation formulation of stochastic behaviour in land use density and rent interactions at the intra-urban level, where the macro-foundation of micro-behaviour and then the micro-foundation of macro-behaviour were laid out.

Complexity can be modelled through the use of simple mathematical models when stability characterizes the system's dynamic behaviour. When enough uniformity is observed at micro-level behaviour, then a stochastic micro-to-macro interacting behaviour model can be successfully replaced, by a deterministic mean value (expected aggregate behaviour) one. Both elements are the building blocks of dynamic theory in the natural sciences. The first is encountered in the simplicity of physical and chemical laws. It was demonstrated by Smale's work in mathematics on stability in dynamical systems (1966), as well as in the work by May (1973) in biology on complexity vs. stability in modelling interacting species. The second is found in the stochastic master equation formulation of dynamical systems in general and specifically the Fokker-Planck equation in quantum theory. The validity of both is documented, through empirical testing, for urban systems as well.

There are profound implications stemming from these findings. Apparently, the nature of the inner structure of interacting systems (their chemistry, physics, biology, economy, sociology) is not as important as the form of their dynamic interaction. This is a major premiss of the structuralist mode of thought put forward by Thom's structural stability theory and echoed by Amson (1975). The outcome of the interaction, for an inside observer, has a structure which is, for the purposes of serving the examination needs of the observer, more profitably linked to the apparent interaction behaviour than the systems' inner nature. The observer can outline the structure of the outcome of their interaction, evidently, without reference to the detailed and precise nature of these systems. The observer can productively use a mathematical (abstract) representation of their apparent indicators of interacting behaviour (outcome) in order to study their evolution.

It turns out that these abstract representations are similar for a large number of such systems, and that they are quite simple. Further, the possible structure of the outcome in dynamically interacting systems contains a very limited and well-defined, observed variety. This is so in spite of the possibly infinite variety of performance. Thus, there is selection present in the behaviour of all urban systems, favouring particular associations. It was found that this selection process favours stability in the macro-urban scale and instability at the intra-urban level in the evolution of metropolitan systems.

This apparent universality of mathematical abstraction along specific lines in dynamical analysis for the study of natural and urban systems is the outcome of a selection process. It identifies a situation in which the observers of various interacting natural and urban systems choose, among the tools available from a standing pool, identical ones. To classify this as mere mimicking would miss the point: it has happened enough times, by too many observers from both sides to characterize it as such. It points towards the simultaneous adoption of a philosophical standpoint. The issue is too large, however, to deal with here. Only few comments will be made in the spirit of the work in this book.

Only during the last century have the social sciences used mathematical tools in their method, late-comers in this respect relative to the natural sciences. One can possibly see them eventually becoming branches of mathematics. What is or has been the kind of interconnectance among the natural sciences, mathematics and the social sciences, and how these links have shaped the evolution of these branches of human inquiry are topics still open to debate and research. Whether a deterministic developmental path exists in the field of mathematics from which the natural and social sciences continuously draw cannot be proven, as one cannot prove that out of necessity the particular developments in these three areas of human inquiry did occur.

But one cannot but notice the coincidences in utilizing the mathematical formalism most recently available (with different time-lags due to the diffusion process) to phenomena in both areas. The detailed nature of the problem seems to be a derivative of the abstract formalism developed, i.e. the scientific method. This particular selection could favour stability, if not at the development of a particular field, but for the overall human quest for improving understanding and knowledge. It may point to a particular developmental path of human inquiry, favouring stability.

Micro-foundations of macro-behaviour can be detected in the evolution of the scientific method. Particular perceptions and foundations of particular natural and social problems, events, and phenomena constitute the dynamics of development in science at large. Scientists adopt particular scientific approaches to particular problems in a manner equivalent to an ecological interconnectance among members of a scientific community. The particular configuration of the scientific community matrix determines the conditions of stability in each discipline and the scientific field as a whole. Micro-behaviour, the attitudes of each scientist or small group of scientists, schools of thought, might have significant effects upon the behaviour of the whole community. In science, the assumption regarding uniformity in behaviour within groups must be indeed extremely strong.

Intellectual innovation occurs with a very high frequency. However innovation is dense at particular time-periods. Viewed from this perspective, selection must favour instability in the development of the fields of human inquiry. It favours high degree of innovation and interconnectance, as connectivity among various scientific groups is highly random. What implications this holds for the future of the area of social sciences in general and the field of urban science in particular, remains to be seen.

APPENDIX I

To illustrate neighbourhood stability analysis in the planar case consider the following example (found in Clark, 1976) of a general *linear* version of the original system

$$\frac{dx}{dt} = f(x)$$

$$\frac{dy}{dt} = g(x)$$

namely

$$\frac{dx}{dt} = ax + by$$

$$\frac{dy}{dt} = cx + dy.$$

Together these differential equations imply

$$\frac{d^2x}{dt^2} = (a + d)\frac{dx}{dt} + (bc - ad)x$$

The expression $C \exp(\lambda t)$ is a solution if

$$\lambda^2 - (a + d)\lambda - (bc - ad) = 0,$$

or $\det(A - \lambda I) = 0$, where A and I are given by

$$A = \begin{bmatrix} a & b \\ c & d \end{bmatrix} \qquad I = \begin{bmatrix} 1 & 0 \\ 0 & 1 \end{bmatrix}$$

If λ_1 and λ_2 are different real roots of the characteristic polynomial, $\det(A - \lambda I) = 0$, then the general solution is given by

$$x(t) = C_{11} \exp(\lambda_1 t) + C_{12} \exp(\lambda_2 t)$$

$$y(t) = C_{21} \exp(\lambda_1 t) + C_{22} \exp(\lambda_2 t).$$

A summary of the possible values for λ_1, λ_2 and the corresponding equilibria is given in Table A.1, while the phase portraits corresponding to these equilibria are shown in Fig. A1.

TABLE A.1.   *Characteristic roots and equilibria of a dynamical system in the plane*

Eigenvalues		Nature of equilibrium
λ_1, λ_2	positive, real, unequal	unstable node
λ_1, λ_2	negative, real, unequal	stable node
λ_1	negative, real	saddle
λ_2	positive, real	
λ_1, λ_2	complex, with positive real part	unstable focus (source spiral)
λ_1, λ_2	complex, with negative real part	stable focus (sink spiral)
λ_1, λ_2	complex, pure imaginary	centre (orbital)

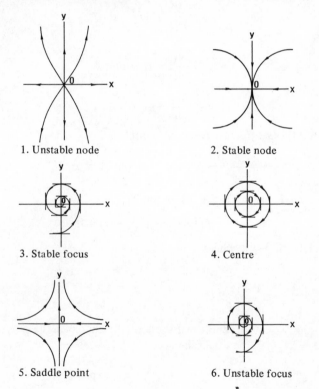

1. Unstable node   2. Stable node

3. Stable focus   4. Centre

5. Saddle point   6. Unstable focus

FIG. A.1.   *Phase portraits of dynamical systems in the plane, linearized around the origin*

APPENDIX II

Here a brief review of the notion of structural stability as employed in catastrophe theory is made, and the cusp catastrophe is presented to set the stage for Zeeman's fast–slow dynamic model.

In mathematical terms, the notion of structural stability may be approached by considering any function with N parameters as occupying a location in N-parameter space. If F_p is the function corresponding to the point P in this space, and if for Q close to P the corresponding function F_q has the same form as F_p, then F_q is called structurally stable or generic function of the family containing F_p. The set of all points whose corresponding functions are generic is the subset of generic points. The complement of this set is the bifurcation set.

To make these rather vague notions more concrete, using Saunders (1980), one can examine the set of polynomials in one variable of degree $\leq N$. Polynomials will be considered to be of the same type if they have the same configuration of critical points near $x = 0$. Compare, for example, the function x^4 with the neighbouring polynomial $W = x^4 + ax^b$. x^4 has a minimum at the origin, and for $b \geq 4$ so does W. If $b = 3$, however, W has an inflection point at the origin and a minimum at $x = -3/4a$. If $b = 2$, $a < 0$, W has a maximum at the origin and a minimum at $\pm \sqrt{(-a/2)}$.

Thus x^4 is not structurally stable, because there are polynomials close to it which are not of the same type. Note that the function $x^4 + ax^3$ can be brought arbitrarily close to x^4 by making $|a|$ small. The additional critical point is at $x = -a$, so making $|a|$ small brings it close to the origin. This cannot happen with the function $x^4 + ax^5$, for here the additional critical point is at $x = -4/5a$ (as $|a| \uparrow \to 0, x \to \infty$).

Clearly the polynomial

$$V = x^4 + ax^3 + bx^2 + cx + d$$

is structurally stable, since it includes all lower-order terms, and it can be proven that adding higher-order terms cannot affect the type. It is not necessary to include all lower-order terms, however, to ensure structural stability. In fact a function such as V can be written without the cubic or constant terms. Thus all types in the family V occur in V^1, where

$$V^1 = x^4 + ax^3 + cx.$$

V^1 is called the unfolding of the singularity x^4. The explanation of these terms is that while x^4 appears to have only one critical point, the generic family which stabilizes it has three. An unfolding like V^1, which has the minimum number of parameters, is called universal.

The above cases concern polynomials, yet the discussion is quite general, since any sufficiently smooth function can be approximated by a Taylor series. Saunders points out that the coefficient of x^N in the Taylor expansion around

$$x = 0 \text{ is } \frac{\mathrm{d}^N F}{\mathrm{d}x^N}(0).$$

The critical points of a function are usually determined by the sign of the second derivative. If this vanishes, one progresses to the next derivative, and so on. If N terms beyond the second derivative can be obtained the function is said to have an N-fold degeneracy, and require N terms to stabilize it. Once a non-vanishing term is found the rest of the series can be ignored.

The Zeeman fast and slow equations

Zeeman in (1972) provides a path-breaking formulation of a recursive process which involves a fast and a slow motion on the surface of a cusp. The particular problem he addresses is the heartbeat and nerve impulse; however, his general formulation can be applied to a variety of contexts. The problem according to Zeeman is to trace the dynamics of the following systems

$$\epsilon \dot{x} = f(x, a, b)$$

$$\dot{a} = g(x, a, b)$$

$$\dot{b} = h(x, a, b)$$

where ϵ is a very small number; x is the fast adjustor, whereas a and b are the slow variables. In the heartbeat problem $\dot{x} = 0$ is a third-order polynomial of x and the surface of the singular points of the cusp catastrophe. Cyclical changes in the control variables $\dot{a}$ and $\dot{b}$ depict an oscillatory motion in the (a, b) space, subject to a discontinuity when the bifurcation set of the cusp catastrophe is crossed during each cycle.

A fast-slow dynamic dichotomy seems to be pervasive in urban and regional systems. Dendrinos and Mullally (1981), for example, employed the Zeeman model to describe the relatively fast motion of urban populations and the relatively slow changes in comparative advantages and developmental costs. Further, inter-urban population-factor reward dynamics (discussed in Part II, E) seem clearly to suggest that in the US, over the time-period surveyed, income (factor reward) obeys a relatively slow dynamic, whereas population level is a fast adjustor.

An interesting extension of the fast-slow formalism would be to recognize that in urban and regional systems one variable may not remain for prolonged time-periods relatively fast in comparison to another, but instead it could trade roles. Population may be a fast adjustor relative to income changes over a particular time-period, whereas then income may become the fast-adjusting variable with population the slow-moving one. It seems that this process of success-ful fast-slow-fast movement could be present in urban and regional development over longer time-spans. This event might be detected in periods characterized by expansion-consolidation-contraction in population and contraction-consolidation-expansion in factor reward correspondingly.

Notions of fast-slow movement can also be incorporated in population-capital stock interaction under absolute growth conditions, equivalent to the ones examined in Part II, Section G.

APPENDIX III

In proving the theorem we follow Volterra (1939, pt. II). The first variation is

$$\delta P = \int_0^t \left\{ [m_1 \ln \frac{dx}{dt} + m_1 - m_2 \, \beta \ln (\alpha - \beta \, \frac{dx}{dt}) - m_2 \beta] \, \frac{d\delta X}{dt} + k\delta X \right\} dt$$

and consequently

$$\delta P = \int_0^t [(-\frac{m_1}{\frac{dX}{dt}} - \frac{m_2 \beta^2}{\alpha - \beta \, \frac{dx}{dt}}) \, \frac{d^2 X}{dt^2} + k] \, \delta X dt.$$

If we insert appropriately in the function F inside the integral

$$m_1 = \beta m_2 > 0 \text{ and } k = \alpha m_1$$

then the Euler condition becomes the Verhulst–Pearl equation

$$\frac{d^2 X}{dt^2} = \frac{dX}{dt} (\alpha - \beta \, \frac{dX}{dt}).$$

for values of $x < \alpha/\beta$ the second variation is positive, the sufficient condition for minimum of the potential. Volterra, in his classical paper 'Calculus of Variations and the Logistic Curve', interprets this as the minimum social energy potential.

Volterra has extended this to a generalized specification of the Verhulst–Pearl equation

$$\frac{dx}{dt} = x \prod_i (\alpha_i - x); \; i = 1, \ldots I$$

where now the integrand $F(t)$ in the potential is

$$F(t) = \sum_i m_i (\alpha_i - x) \ln (\alpha_i - x) + kX.$$

Note its entropic form $(\alpha_i - x) \ln (\alpha_i - x)$. Next, the case of a multiple species, conservative association, potential is given. Volterra analysed the case where

$$\dot{x}_i = x_i(a_i^0 - \frac{1}{b_i} \sum_j a_j^i x_j)$$

and introducing the potential

$$V = \sum_i \alpha_i x_i.$$

Total differential of V is

$$dV = \sum_i d_i a_i^0 x \, dt - \sum_i \sum_j \frac{1}{b_i} a_j^i a_i^0 x_i x_j \, dt.$$

Conservation by Volterra implies that the second term of the r.h.s. is zero. He called this term 'total species interaction'. The interaction matrix $A = \| a_{ij} \|$ must be antisymmetric

$$a_j^i = - a_i^j \text{ and } a_i^i = 0.$$

Volterra's canonical form of the potential giving rise to the original differential equation on $\dot{x}_i$ is the integrand

$$F = \sum_i b_i \dot{X}_i \ln \dot{X}_i + \sum_i \sum_j a_j^i X_i X_j - \sum_i a_i^0 b_i \dot{X}$$

where $X_i = \int_0^t \dot{x}_i dt$.

Designating as x_i^* the equilibrium state then, Volterra shows

$$\prod_i \left[(e^{X_i}) \Big/ x_i x_i^* \right]^{b_i} = C'$$

where C' is a constant. This is the well-known Volterra first integral for the system

$$\dot{x}_i = x_i(a_i^0 + \frac{1}{b_i} \sum_j a_j^i x_j).$$

APPENDIX IV

The specification for the utility model are as follows

$$f = \dot{U} = x(a - bx) - cU$$

$$g = \dot{x} = \alpha(\bar{U} - U)$$

so that the equilibria are given by the intersection of the two isoclines

$$U^0 = \frac{1}{c}x^0(a - bx^0); \quad x^0 < \frac{a}{b}$$

$$U^{00} = \bar{U}.$$

Global maximum of U is obtained at

$$\frac{\partial U^0}{\partial x} = 0 \rightarrow \frac{1}{c}(a - 2bx) = 0 \rightarrow \bar{x} = \frac{a}{2b}$$

$$U_{max} = \frac{a^2}{4bc} \quad \text{with} \quad \frac{\partial^2 U^0}{\partial x^2} = -2b/c < 0.$$

The two intersections occur at

$$(\bar{U}, x_i^*) = [\bar{U}, \frac{a - \sqrt{(a^2 - 4bc\bar{U})}}{2b}] \text{ and } (\bar{U}, x_2^*) = [\bar{U}, \frac{a + \sqrt{(a^2 - 4bc\bar{U})}}{2b}]$$

where their respective stability conditions require that the characteristic polynomial (at the equilibrium points x_1^*, x_2^*)

$$\begin{bmatrix} f_U^* - \lambda & g_U^* \\ f_x^* & g_x^* - \lambda \end{bmatrix} = \begin{bmatrix} -c - \lambda & -\alpha \\ \pm\sqrt{(a^2 - 4bc\bar{U})} & -\lambda \end{bmatrix} = 0.$$

The eigenvalues' real parts must be negative

$$f_U^* + g_x^* < 0 \rightarrow -c < 0$$

and

$$f_U^* g_x^* - f_x^* g_U^* > 0 \rightarrow \alpha[\pm\sqrt{(a^2 - 4bc\bar{U})}] > 0.$$

The first requires that $c > 0$ whereas the second is only satisfied at x_2^*. Thus the x_2^* is a stable whereas the x_1^* is an unstable equilibrium. A fourth-degree polynomial on x of the f isocline will produce the case of Fig. II.2. This can be obtained by introducing city size into the utility function.

APPENDIX V

These qualitative properties are contained in the urban matrix A of the linearized system. In matrix notation and by dropping the distinction in notation between x and y we obtain

$$\dot{z} = Az$$

the urban Jacobian square matrix A has dimensions $2I$ by $2I$ with entries (asterisk denoting equilibrium)

$$\alpha_{kl} = \frac{\partial H_k}{\partial z_1} z_1^*,$$

where, $k, l = 1, 2, \ldots, 2I$. The urban matrix A can be partitioned into parts representing: A_{11} the population-to-population; A_{12} population-to-reward; A_{21} reward-to-population; A_{22} reward-to-reward interactions, for any pair of cities

$$A = \begin{bmatrix} A^{11} & | & A^{12} \\ -- & | & -- \\ A^{21} & | & A^{22} \end{bmatrix}$$

As the differential equations are linear in z the solution of the system is

$$z_k(t) = \sum_1 C_{kl} \exp(\lambda_1 t)$$

where λ_1 are the $2I$ eigenvalues of the characteristic polynomial, and C_{kl} are constants which depend on the initial values of x and y. The eigenvalues are obtained by solving the system

$$(A - \lambda I)z = 0$$

I being the identity matrix. It has a non-trivial solution if and only if the determinant is zero. If the eigenvalues have positive real parts then the real part of the root produces exponential growth, whereas its imaginary part produces oscillations. Zero real part is associated with cycles.

APPENDIX VI

From the specifications, following Volterra (1926, pt. II):

$$\dot{z}_1 = z_1 \left(a_1 - \sum_k b_{1k} z_k \right)$$

$$F(z_1, z_2 \ldots, z_{2I}) = \sum_1^{2I} \sum_k^{2I} \alpha_1 b_{1k} z_k z_1$$

it follows that

$$\sum_1 \alpha_1 \dot{z}_1 = \sum_1 \alpha_1 a_1 z_1 - F$$

and substituting x and y

$$\sum_i \alpha_i \dot{x}_i + \sum_i \beta_i \dot{y}_i = \sum_i \alpha_i a_i x_i + \sum_i \beta_i b_i y_i - F.$$

Set $x_{i^0} = 1$ and $y_{i^0} = 1$ and denote by m_i and n_i (both positive) the lower limit of the values of F for all possible values of $x_1, \ldots x_I$; and $y_1, \ldots y_I$. Let m and n be the smallest of the numbers of $m_1, \ldots m_I$ and $n_1, \ldots n_I$ and let

$$\sum_i | \alpha_i a_i | < E_1$$

$$\sum_i | \beta_i b_i | < E_2.$$

Suppose that from a certain time t_1, x_{i^0} remains larger than $E_1 + 1$ and y_{i^0} remains larger than $E_2 + 1$. Denote by $M_1(t_2)$ the largest of the numbers $x_1(t_2), \ldots x_I(t_2)$ and by $M_2(t_2)$ the largest of the numbers $y_1(t_2) \ldots, y_I(t_2)$ when $t_2 > t_1$. We have

$$F_{t=t_2} > m M_1{}^2(t_2) + n M_2{}^2(t_2)$$

$$\sum_i \alpha_i a_i x_i(t_2) < E_1 M_1(t_2)$$

$$\sum_i \beta_i b_i y_i(t_2) < E_2 M_2(t_2).$$

From the above we obtain

$$\left(\sum_i \alpha_i \dot{x}_i\right)_{t=t_2} + \left(\sum_i \beta_i \dot{y}_i\right)_{t=t_2} > [E_1 - mM_1(t_2)] M_1(t_2)$$
$$+ [E_2 - nM_2(t_2)] M_2(t_2)$$

However,

$$M_1(t_2) > \frac{E_1 + 1}{m} \text{ and } M_2(t_2) > \frac{E_2 + 1}{n}$$

thus

$$\left(\sum_i \alpha_i \dot{x}_i\right)_{t=t_2} + \left(\sum_i \beta \dot{y}\right)_{t=t_2} < -\left(\frac{E_1 + 1}{m} + \frac{E_2 + 1}{n}\right)$$

so that x and/or y must become negative, which contradicts the original assumptions of positivity.

APPENDIX VII

Volterra, in (1926, pt. II) examined the multiple species case when the F function in the system:

$$\dot{x}_1 = z_1 \cdot F_1(z_1, \ldots z_1)$$

is linear. His analysis can easily be extended to the urban ecological case. Assume that

$$\dot{z}_1 = z_1(a_1 + b_1 F)$$

where z can be either population or reward accumulation. For two particular accumulations the above becomes

$$\dot{z}_1 = z_1 a_1 + z_1 b_1 F$$
$$\dot{z}_k = z_k a_k + z_k b_k F$$

where F is the same function within the sets of rewards or population accumulations, but not between the two. Then if z_l and z_k represent populations of towns l and k

$$\frac{\dot{z}_l}{b_l z_l} - \frac{a_l}{b_l} = \frac{\dot{z}_k}{b_k z_k} - \frac{a_k}{b_k}$$

and by integrating, switching from logarithms to numbers, one obtains

$$z_l^{\frac{1}{b_l}} \Big/ z_k^{\frac{1}{b_k}} = C \exp \left[\left(\frac{a_l}{b_l} - \frac{a_k}{b_k}\right) t \right]$$

where C is some positive constant. If one orders the ratios a_l/b_l in a descending order of magnitude so that

$$\frac{a_1}{b_1} > \frac{a_2}{b_2} > \ldots \frac{a_I}{b_I}$$

and $l < k$, then

$$\lim_{t \to \infty} \frac{z_l^{\frac{1}{b_l}}}{z_k^{\frac{1}{b_k}}} = \infty.$$

This requires that as one looks at the very long run, either city l will grow to be extremely large, or city k will become extinct.

APPENDIX VIII

The general Volterra–Lotka system

$$\dot{x} = \alpha(a^0 + a^1 x + a^2 w)x \ (=f)$$
$$\dot{w} = \beta(b^0 + b^1 x + b^2 w)w \ (=g)$$

has isoclines given by

$$a^0 + a^1 x + a^2 w = 0$$
$$b^0 + b^1 x + b^2 w = 0.$$

By Cramer's rule one obtains the equilibrium x^*, w^*

$$x^* = \frac{a^2 b^0 - a^0 b^2}{a^1 b^2 - a^2 b^1}, \qquad w^* = \frac{a^0 b^1 - a^1 b^0}{a^1 b^2 - a^2 b^1}$$

if the determinant does not vanish. The intra-zonal, inter-activity matrix is

$$A = \begin{bmatrix} \alpha a^1 x^* - \lambda & \alpha a^2 x^* \\ \beta b^1 w^* & \beta b^2 w^* - \lambda \end{bmatrix}$$

where the entries are f_x, f_w, g_x and g_w of the linearized system at x^*, w^* and λ are the roots of the characteristic polynomial, i.e. the system's eigenvalues. Conditions for stability require that at x^*, w^*

$$f_x + g_w < 0 \text{ and}$$
$$f_x g_w - f_w g_x > 0.$$

Spiralling motion occurs when for x^*, w^*

$$(f_x - g_w)^2 + 4 f_w g_x > 0.$$

Since under predation $f_w \cdot g_x < 0$, the relative magnitude of the left-hand side of the above condition would depend on the relative slopes (a^1/a^2 and b^1/b^2) of the two isoclines. In Fig. II.2 where the spiralling attractors are shown, this condition is assumed to be met.

APPENDIX IX

The mathematical description is provided here of the dynamic master equation formulation of the rent-density interaction in two zones within a metropolitan area. In Haag and Dendrinos (1983) a full exposition is shown of the mathematical analysis involved in deriving the mean value deterministic equation from the stochastic master equation.

In two zones i and j of land area z_i and z_j, average population densities n_i and n_j are observed so that

$$n_i z_i = N + n$$
$$n_j z_j = N - n.$$

Average rents in these two zones satisfy the conditions:

$$r_i z_i = R + r$$
$$r_j z_j = R - r$$

with $-N \leq n \leq N$ and $-R \leq r \leq R$ where N and R are known and fixed. A typical resident of these two zones migrates according to an exponential probability function

$$u_{j \rightarrow i} = \alpha \exp a_1 \left((\bar{r}_i - r_i) - (\bar{r}_j - r_j) + a_2 (n_i - n_j) \right) = \alpha e^{U_{j \rightarrow i}}$$
$$U_{i \rightarrow j} = -U_{j \rightarrow i}$$

where $\bar{r}$ denotes bid-rent. At the same time relative rental value flows from i to j according to the exponential function

$$v_{j \rightarrow i} = \beta \exp a_3 \left((n_i - \bar{n}_i) - (n_j - \bar{n}_j) \right) = \beta e^{V_{j \rightarrow i}}$$
$$V_{j \rightarrow i} = -V_{i \rightarrow j}$$

where $\bar{n}_i$ and $\bar{n}_j$ are carrying capacities. In the aggregate, the system moves to a neighbouring state by the following conditions

$$w(n+1, r; n, r) = n_j z_j \alpha \exp U_{j \rightarrow i}$$
$$w(n-1, r; n, r) = n_i z_i \alpha \exp (-U_{j \rightarrow i})$$

$$w\,(n,r+1;n,r) \;=\; r_j z_j \beta \exp V_{j\to i}$$

$$w\,(n,r-1;n,r) \;=\; r_i z_i \beta \exp -(V_{j\to i})$$

with all $w\,[\;\;] \geq 0$. The stochastic master equation of the two-zone density–rent problem is

$$\frac{\mathrm{d}P(n,r;t)}{\mathrm{d}t} =$$

$$w\,(n,r;n+1,r)\;P\,(n+1,r;t)\;-\;w\,(n-1,r;n,r)\;P\,(n,r;t)$$

$$+\;w\,(n,r,n-1,r)\;P\,(n-1,r;t)\;-\;w\,(n+1,r;n,r)\;P\,(n,r;t)$$

$$+\;w\,(n,r;n,r+1)\;P\,(n,r+1;t)\;-\;w\,(n,r-1;n,r)\;P\,(n,r;t)$$

$$+\;w\,(n,r;n,r-1)\;P\,(n,r-1;t)\;-\;w\,(n,r+1;n,r)\;P\,(n,r;t).$$

Defining $x = n/N$ and $y = r/R$ the mean value equations are obtained

$$\dot{x} = \alpha \sinh (b_0 - b_1 y + b_2 x) - \cosh (b_0 - b_1 y + b_2 x)$$

$$\dot{y} = \beta \sinh (-b_3 + b_4 x) - y \cosh (-b_3 + b_4 x)$$

where,

$$b_0 = a_1 (\bar{r}_i - \bar{r}_j) - (a_1 R - a_2 N)\,(\frac{1}{z_i} - \frac{1}{z_j})$$

$$b_1 = R\,a_1 (\frac{1}{z_i} + \frac{1}{z_j})$$

$$b_2 = N\,a_2 (\frac{1}{z_i} + \frac{1}{z_j})$$

$$b_3 = a_3\,[(\bar{n}_i - \bar{n}_j) + N\,(\frac{1}{z_i} - \frac{1}{z_i})]$$

$$b_4 = a_3\,(\frac{1}{z_i} + \frac{1}{z_j}).$$

In order to derive these deterministic mean value equations, one must assume that only one peak exists in the master equation, so that if by bar one denotes mean value, then

$$\frac{\mathrm{d}\bar{n}}{\mathrm{d}t} \;\eqsim\; K_n\,(\bar{n}, \bar{r})$$

$$\frac{\mathrm{d}\bar{r}}{\mathrm{d}t} \;\eqsim\; K_r\,(\bar{n}, \bar{r})$$

where

$$K_n(n,r) = w[n + 1, r; n,r] - w[n - 1, r; n,r]$$
$$K_r(n,r) = w[n,r + 1; n,r] - w[n,r - 1; n,r]$$

and similarly for the rental part of the equation. The twelve US SMSAs used to calibrate and test the model are: Buffalo, NY; Philadelphia, Pa.; Pittsburgh, Pa.; Portland, Ore.; San Diego, Calif.; Spokane, Wa.; Atlantic City, NJ; Erie, Pa.; Miami, Fla.; Altoona, Pa.; Omaha, Nebr.; Trenton, NJ. With the exception of α, β all other parameters were assumed to be identical for all SMSAs and to remain constant over time.

REFERENCES

Allen, P. and Sanglier, M. (1981). 'A Dynamic Model of a Central Place System', *Geographical Analysis*, Vol. 13, no. 2, 149–64.
–, Deneubourg, J. L., Sanglier, M., DePalma, A. (1978). 'The Dynamics of Urban Evolution', Vol. 1: Interurban evolution; Vol. 2: Intraurban evolution, *Final Report to the US Department of Transportation*, Washington, DC.
Alonso, W. (1964). *Location and Land Use* (Cambridge, Mass.: Harvard University Press).
Amson, J. (1972). 'Equilibrium Models of Cities: 1. An Axiomatic Theory', *Environment and Planning*, Vol. 4, 429–44.
– (1973). 'Equilibrium Models of Cities: 2. Single Species Cities', *Environment and Planning*, Vol. 5, 295–338.
– (1975). 'Catastrophe Theory: A Contribution to the Study of Urban Systems?', *Environment and Planning B*, Vol. 2, 177–221.

Beckmann, M. (1952). 'A Continuous Model of Transportation', *Econometrica*, Vol. 20, 643–60.
– (1957). 'On the Distribution of Rent and Residential Density in Cities', paper presented at the Inter-Departmental Seminar on Mathematical Applications in the Social Sciences, Yale University.
Bennett, R. (1980). 'Dynamic Modelling and Control in Urban and Regional Planning', paper presented at the NSF/DOT Conference on 'Nonlinear Dynamic Urban and Regional Theory', Washington, DC, May.
Berlinski, D. (1976). *On Systems Analysis*. (Cambridge, Mass.: MIT Press).
Berry, B. (1967). *Geography of Market Centers and Retail Distribution* (Englewood Cliffs, N.J.: Prentice-Hall).
– and Kasarda, J. (1977). *Contemporary Urban Ecology* (New York: Macmillan).
Brauer, F. (1979). 'Boundedness of Solutions of Predator-prey Systems', *Journal of Theoretical Population Biology*, Vol. 15, 268–73.
Brillouin, L. (1962). *Science and Information Theory* (London: Academic Press).
Bulmer, M. G. (1976). 'The Theory of Predator-prey Oscillations', *Journal of Theoretical Population Biology*, Vol. 9, 137–50.

Casetti, E. (1981). 'A Catastrophe Model of Regional Dynamics', *Annals of the American Association of Geographers*, Vol. 71, no. 4, 572–9.

Casti, J. (1979). *Connectivity, Complexity and Catastrophe in Large-Scale Systems* (New York: John Wiley).

— (1982). 'Topological Methods for Social and Behavioral Systems', *International Journal of General Systems*, Vol. 8, 187–210.

Chesson, P. (1978). 'Predator-prey Theory and Variability', *Annual Review of Ecological Systems*, Vol. 9, 323–48.

Christaller, W. (1933). *Central Places in Southern Germany*, translated by C. W. Baskin (Englewood Cliffs, NJ: Prentice-Hall).

Clark, C. (1976) *Mathematical Bioeconomics* (New York: John Wiley).

Clarke, M. and Wilson, A. (1983). 'The Dynamics of Urban Spatial Structure: Progress and Problems', *Journal of Regional Science*, Vol. 23, no. 1, 1–18.

Cobb, L. (1981). 'Parameter Estimation for the Cusp Catastrophe', *Behavioral Science*, Vol. 26, 75–8.

Consortium of Authors (1983). 'Theory in the Social Sciences', *Geographical Analysis*, Vol. 15, no. 1, 28–75.

Cronin, J. (1977). 'Some Mathematics of Biological Oscillators', *SIAM Review*, Vol. 19, no. 1 (January), 100–38.

Cruz, J. B. (1980). 'Models for Pluralistic Decision-Making in Urban and Regional Systems', mimeo University of Illinois, Department of Electrical Engineering, Champaign-Urbana.

Curry, L. (1981). 'Division of Labor from Geographical Competition', *Annals of the Association of American Geographers*, Vol. 71, no. 2 (June), 133–65.

Day, R. (1982). 'Irregular Growth Cycles', *American Economic Review*, Vol. 72, no. 3, 406–14.

Dendrinos, D. S. (1976). 'Two Applications of Catastrophe Theory in Transportation Planning and Urban Economics', paper presented at the 23rd Annual Meeting of the Regional Science Association, Toronto.

— (1978). 'Urban Dynamics and Urban Cycles', *Environment and Planning A*, Vol. 10, 43–9.

— (1979). 'A Basic Model of Urban Dynamics Expressed as a Set of Volterra-Lotka Equations', in D. S. Dendrinos, *Catastrophe Theory in Urban and Transport Analysis*, Report #DOT/RSPA/DPB-25/80/20, US Department of Transportation, Washington, DC, June 1980, 79–103.

— (1980a). *Catastrophe Theory in Urban and Transport Analysis*, Report # DOT/RSPA/DPB-25/80/20, US Department of Transportation, Washington, DC, June.

Dendrinos, D. S. (1980b). 'Dynamics of City Size and Structural Stability: the Case of a Single City', *Geographical Analysis*, Vol. 12, no. 3, 236-44.

— (1983). 'Epistemological Aspects of Metropolitan Evolution', in B. Crosby (ed.), *Cities and Regions as Nonlinear Decision Systems* (Westview Press).

— (1984a). 'Regions, Antiregions and their Dynamic Stability: the Case of the US (1929-1979)', *Journal of Regional Science*, Vol. 24, no. 1, 65-83.

— (1984b). 'On the Structural Stability of US Regions: Some Theoretical Underpinnings', *Environment and Planning A*, November 1984.

— (1984c). 'Turbulence in Urban/Regional Dynamics', paper presented at the Annual Meeting of the American Association of Geographers, Washington, DC, April.

— (1984d). 'Madrid's Aggregate Growth Pattern: A Note on the Evidence Regarding the Urban Volterra-Lotka Model', *Sistemi Urbani*, Vol. VI, No. 3, November 1984.

— and Haag, G. (1983). 'Toward a Stochastic Dynamical Theory of Location: Empirical Evidence', *Geographical Analysis*, Vol. 16, no. 4: 287-300

— and Mullally, H. (1981). 'Fast and Slow Equations: the Development Patterns of Urban Settings', *Environment and Planning A*, Vol. 13, 819-27.

— (1982a). 'Evolutionary Patterns of Metropolitan Populations', *Geographical Analysis*, Vol. 13, no. 4, 328-44.

— (1982b). 'Empirical Evidence of Volterra-Lotka Dynamics in US Metropolitan Areas: 1940-1977', in D. Griffith, T. Lea (eds.), *Evolving Geographical Structures*, Martinus Nijhoff, 1983: 170-95.

— (1983). 'Optimum Control of Nonlinear Ecological Dynamics in Metropolitan Areas', *Environment and Planning A*, Vol. 15, 543-50.

— and Sonis, M. (1984). 'Variational Principles and Conservation Conditions in Volterra's Ecology and in Urban Relative Dynamics', paper presented at the Second International Congress of Regional Science, Rotterdam, June.

Emlen, J.M. (1973). *Ecology, An Evolutionary Approach* (Reading: Addison-Wesley).

Feigenbaum, M. (1980). 'Universal Behavior in Nonlinear Systems', *Los Alamos Science*, Summer 2-27.

Fisk, C. S. and Boyce, D. E. (1983). 'Decision-making in the Planning and Operation of Transportation Systems', *Environment and Planning A*, Vol. 15, 556-7.

Forrester, J. (1971). *Urban Dynamics* (Cambridge, Mass.: MIT Press).

Gardner, M. R. and Ashby, W. R. (1970). 'Connections of Large Dynamical (cybernetic) Systems: Critical Values for Stability', *Nature*, Vol. 228, 784.

Gilmore, R. (1981). *Catastrophe Theory for Scientists and Engineers* (New York: Wiley-Interscience).

Gilpin, M. E. (1979). 'Spiral Chaos in a Predator-prey Model', *American Naturalist*, Vol. 113, 306-8.

Goel, N. S., Maitra, S. C., and Montroll, E. W. (1971). *On the Volterra and Other Nonlinear Models of Interacting Populations* (London: Academic Press).

Goh, B. S. (1969). 'Optimal Control of a Fish Resource', *Malayan Scientist*, Vol. 5, 65-70.

Gurel, O. and Rossler, O. (1979). *Bifurcation Theory and Applications in Scientific Disciplines*, Annals of the New York Academy of Sciences, Vol. 316, February.

Haag, G. and Dendrinos, D. S. (1983). 'Toward a Stochastic Dynamical Theory of Location: A Nonlinear Migration Process', *Geographical Analysis*, Vol. 15, no. 4, 269-86.

Harris, B. (1965). 'A Model of Locational Equilibrium for the Retail Trade', mimeo, Institute for Urban Studies, University of Pennsylvania.

— and Wilson, A. (1978). 'Equilibrium Values and Dynamics of Attractiveness Terms in Production-Constrained Spatial-Interaction Models', *Environment and Planning A*, Vol. 10, 371-88.

Hayek, F. A. von (1975). 'The Pretence of Knowledge', *Swedish Journal of Economics*, Vol. 77, No. 4: 433-42

Henderson, J. M. and Quandt, R. E. (1971). *Microeconomic Theory: A Mathematical Approach* (New York: McGraw-Hill).

Henderson, J. V. (1977). *Economic Theory and the Cities*, (London: Academic Press).

Hill, D. (1965). 'A Growth Allocation Model for the Boston Region', *Journal of the American Institute of Planners*, Vol. 31, 111-20.

Hirsch, M. and Smale, S. (1974). *Differential Equations, Dynamical Systems, and Linear Algebra* (London: Academic Press).

Hotelling, H. (1929). 'Stability in Competition', *Economic Journal*, Vol. 29, 41-57.

Hoyt, H. (1933). *One Hundred Years of Land Values in Chicago* (Chicago, Ill.: University of Chicago Press).

Hutchinson, G. E. (1978). *An Introduction to Population Ecology* New Haven: Yale University Press).

Ingram, G., Kain, J., and Ginn, R. (1972). *The Detroit Prototype of the*

NBER Urban Simulation Model (New York: Columbia University Press).

Intriligator, M. D. (1971). *Mathematical Optimization and Economic Theory* (Englewood Cliffs, NJ: Prentice-Hall).

Isard, W. (1975). *Introduction to Regional Science* (Englewood Cliffs, NJ: Prentice-Hall).

Jacobs, J. (1969). *The Economy of Cities* (Vintage).

Jeffries, C. (1974). 'Qualitative Stability and Digraphs in Model Ecosystems', *Ecology*, Vol. 55, 1415-19.

Kolmogoroff, A. N. (1936). 'On Volterra's Theory of the Struggle for Existence', in F. Scudo and J. Ziegler (ed.) *The Golden Age of Theoretical Ecology: 1923-1940*, Springer-Verlag. *Lecture Notes in Biomathematics* (1978), Vol. 22, 287-92.

Li, T. Y. and Yorke, J. A. (1975). 'Period Three Implies Chaos', *American Mathematical Monthly*, Vol. 82, 985-92.

Losch, A. (1937). *The Economics of Location*, translated by W. Woglom and W. A. Stopler (New Haven, Conn.: Yale University Press).

Lotka, A. (1932). 'The Growth of Mixed Populations: Two Species Competing for a Common Food Supply', in F. Scudo, J. Ziegler (ed.), *The Golden Age of Theoretical Ecology: 1923-1940*, Springer-Verlag, *Lecture Notes in Biomathematics* (1978), Vol. 22, 274-86.

Lowry, I. (1964). *A Model of Metropolis* (Santa Monica, Calif.: Rand Corporation).

MacArthur, R. H. (1972). *Geographical Ecology* (New York, NY: Harper and Row).

— and Wilson, E. O. (1967). *The Theory of Island Biogeography* (Princeton, NJ: Princeton University Press.

Marsden, J. E., McCracken, M. (1976). *The Hopf Bifurcation and Its Applications*. (Berlin: Springer-Verlag).

May, R. M. (1971). 'Stability in Multi-Species Community Models', *Mathematical Biosciences*, Vol. 12, 59-79.

— (1973). *Stability and Complexity in Model Ecosystems* (Princeton, NJ: Princeton University Press).

— (1974). 'Biological Populations with Nonoverlapping Generations: Stable Points, Stable Cycles and Chaos', *Science*, Vol. 186, 645-7.

— (1975). 'Biological Populations Obeying Difference Equations: Stable Points, Stable Cycles and Chaos', *Journal of Theoretical Biology*, Vol. 49, 511-24.

— (1976). Simple Mathematical Models with Very Complicated Dynamics', *Nature*, Vol. 261, 459-67.

May, R. M. (1979). 'Bifurcations and Dynamic Complexity in Ecological Systems', *Annals of the N.Y. Academy of Sciences*, Vol. 316, 517–29.
– (ed.) (1981). *Theoretical Ecology: Principles and Applications*, 2nd ed. (Sunderland, Mass.: Sinauer Associates).
– and Oster, G. F. (1976). 'Bifurcations and Dynamic Complexity in Simple Ecological Models', *American Naturalist*, Vol. 110, 573–99.
Mees, A. (1975). 'The Revival of Cities in Medieval Europe', *Journal of Regional Science and Urban Economics*, Vol. 5, no. 4, 402–26.
Mehra, R. (1980). 'Experiences with Some Computational Methods and Engineering Applications of Bifurcation Analysis and Catastrophe Theory', paper presented at the NSF/DOT Conference on 'Nonlinear Dynamic Urban and Regional Theory', Washington, DC, May.
Mills, E. (1972). *Studies in the Structure of the Urban Economy* (Baltimore, Md.: Johns Hopkins University Press).
Miyao, T. (1981). *Dynamic Analysis of the Urban Economies* (New York: Academic Press).
Muth, R. (1969). *Cities and Housing* (Chicago, Ill.: Chicago University Press).

Nicolis, G., Prigogine, I. (1977). *Self-organization in Nonequilibrium Systems*, (New York: NY: Wiley).
Nijkamp, P. (1982). 'Long Waves or Catastrophes in Regional Development', *Socio-Economic Planning Sciences*, Vol. 16, 261–71.
Nisbet, R. M. and Gurney, W. S. C. (1982). *Modelling Fluctuating Populations* (New York, NY: Wiley).

Orishimo, I. (1980). 'A Model of Urbanization Process: An Application of Elementary Catastrophe Theory', mimeo, (Tempoku, Japan: Toyohashi University of Technology, Department of Economics).

Pack, J. (1978). *Urban Models: Diffusion and Policy Application:* Monograph Series No. 7, Regional Science Research Institute, University of Pennsylvania.
Paine, R. T. (1980). 'Food Webs: Interaction Strength and Community Infrastructure', *Journal of Animal Ecology*, Vol. 49, 667–85.
– and Levin, S. A. (1981). 'Intertidal Landscapes: Disturbance and the Dynamics of Pattern,' *Ecological Monographs*, Vol. 51, 145–78.
Papageorgiou, Y. Y. (1982). 'Some Thoughts about Theory in the Social Sciences', *Geographical Analysis*, Vol. 14, no. 4, 340–6.
Pavlidis, T. (1973). *Biological Oscillators: Their Mathematical Analysis* (New York, NY: Academic Press).
Pielou, E. C. (1975). *Ecological Diversity*, (New York, NY: John Wiley).

Pimm, S. (1982) *Food Webs*, (London: Chapman & Hall).

Poston, T. and Stewart, I. (1978). *Catastrophe Theory and its Applications* (Belmont, Calif.: Fearon-Pitman).

Puu, T. (1979). 'Regional Modelling and Structural Stability', *Environment and Planning A*, Vol. 11, 1432-8.

Rapport, D. J. and Turner, J. E. (1977). 'Economic Models in Ecology', *Science*, Vol. 195, 367-73.

Roughgarden, J. (1979). *Theory of Population Genetics and Evolutionary Ecology: An Introduction*, (New York, NY: Macmillan).

Samuelson, P. A. (1948). *Foundations of Economic Analysis*. (Cambridge, Mass.: Harvard University Press).

– (1971). 'Generalized Predator-Prey Oscillations in Ecological and Economic Equilibrium', *Proceedings of the National Academy of Sciences*, Vol. 68, 980-3.

Saunders, P. (1980). *Catastrophe Theory* (Cambridge, Eng.: Cambridge University Press).

Schaffer, W. M. (1981). 'Ecological Abstraction: The Consequences of Reduced Dimensionality in Ecological Models', *Ecological Monographs*, Vol. 51, 383-401.

Scudo, F. and Ziergler, J. (ed.) (1978). *The Golden Age of Theoretical Ecology: 1923-1940* (Berlin: Springer-Verlag); *Lecture Notes in Biomathematics*, 22.

Shannon, C. and Weaver, W. (1949). *The Mathematical Theory of Communication* (Urbana, Ill.: University of Illinois Press).

Simmons, J. (1982). Private correspondence.

Simpson, E. H. (1949). 'Measurement of Diversity', *Nature*, Vol. 163, 688.

Slobodkin, L. B. (1961). *Growth and Regulation of Animal Population* (New York, NY.: Holt, Rinehart & Winston).

Smale, S. (1966). 'Structurally Stable Systems are not Dense', *American Journal of Mathematics*, Vol. 87, 491-6.

– (1979). 'On Comparative Statics and Bifurcation in Economic Equilibrium Theory', in O. Gurel and O. E. Rossler (eds.), *Bifurcation Theory and Applications in Scientific Disciplines*, Annals of the New York Academy of Sciences, Vol. 316, Feb.

Smith, J. M. (1974). *Models in Ecology* (Cambridge, Eng.: Cambridge University Press).

Solow, R. (1970). *Growth Theory: An Exposition* (Oxford: Oxford University Press).

Sonis, M. (1983). 'Competition and Environment – A Theory of Temporal Innovation Diffusion', in D. Griffith, A. Lea (eds.) *Evolving Geographic Structures* (The Hague: Martinus Nijhoff).

Szego, G. (1982). *New Quantitative Techniques for Economic Analysis* (New York, NY: Academic Press).

Thom, R. (1975). *Structural Stability and Morphogenesis* (Reading, Mass.: W. A. Benjamin, Inc.).
Thunen, J. H. von (1826). *Der isolierte Staat in Beziehung auf Landwirtschaft und Nationalekonomie*, Hamburg.

US Department of Transportation (1969). *Standard Land Use Coding Manual* (Washington, DC: FHWA).

Volterra, V. (1926). 'Variations and Fluctuations in the Numbers of Coexisting Animal Species', in F. Scudo, J. Ziegler (eds), *The Golden Age of Theoretical Ecology: 1923-1940* (Berlin: Springer-Verlag); *Lecture Notes in Biomathematics*, 22 (1978).
– (1939). 'Calculus of Variations and the Logistic Curve', in F. Scudo, J. Ziegler (eds.), *The Golden Age of Theoretical Ecology: 1923-1940* (Berlin: Springer-Verlag); *Lecture Notes in Biomathematics*, Vol. 22 (1978), 11–17.

Ward, P. M. (1981). 'Mexico City', in M. Pacione (ed.), *Problems and Planning in the Third World Cities* (New York, NY: St Martin's Press).
Watt, K. E. F. (1965). 'Community Stability and the Strategy of Biological Control', *Canadian Entomologist*, Vol. 97, 887–95.
Weidlich, W. and Haag, G. (1980). 'Migration Behavior of Mixed Population in a Town', *Collective Phenomena*, Vol. 3, 89–102.
– (1983). *Concepts and Models of Quantitative Sociology: the Dynamics of Interacting Populations* (Berlin: Springer-Verlag, Series in Synergetics).
Wheaton, W. C. (1974). 'A Comparative Static Analysis of Urban Spatial Structure', *Journal of Economic Theory*, Vol. 9, 223–37.
Whittaker, R. H., Levin, S. A. and Root, R. B. (1973). 'Niche, Habitat, and Ecotope', *American Naturalist*, Vol. 107, 321–38.
Williamson, M. (1972). *The Analysis of Biological Populations* (London: Edward Arnold).
Wilson, A. G. (1970). *Entropy in Urban and Regional Modelling* (London: Pion).
– (1981). *Catastrophe Theory and Bifurcation. Applications to Urban and Regional Systems* (London: Croom Helm).
Woodcock, A. E. R. and Poston, T. (1974). *A Geometrical Study of Elementary Catastrophes* (Berlin: Springer-Verlag); *Lecture Notes in Mathematics*, Vol. 373.

Zeeman, F. C. (1972). 'Differential Equations for the Heartbeat and Nerve Impulse', in C. H. Waddington (ed.), *Towards a Theoretical Biology* (Edinburgh: Edinburgh University Press), Vol. 4, 8–67.
— (1977). *Catastrophe Theory: Selected Papers, 1972-1977* (Reading, Mass.: Addison-Wesley).

INDEX OF AUTHORS

SUBJECT INDEX